W9-BNO-536

CLARA BARTON

Other titles in the **Americans: The Spirit of a Nation** *series:*

ABRAHAM LINCOLN
"This Nation Shall Have a New Birth of Freedom"
ISBN-13: 978-0-7660-3170-8
ISBN-10:   0-7660-3170-5

EDGAR ALLAN POE
"Deep Into That Darkness Peering"
ISBN-13: 978-0-7660-3020-6
ISBN-10:   0-7660-3020-2

MATHEW BRADY
"The Camera Is the Eye of History"
ISBN-13: 978-0-7660-3023-7
ISBN-10:   0-7660-3023-7

CLARA BARTON

"Face Danger, But Never Fear It"

Don Nardo

Enslow Publishers, Inc.
40 Industrial Road
Box 398
Berkeley Heights, NJ 07922
USA

http://www.enslow.com

Library of Congress Cataloging-in-Publication Data:

Nardo, Don, 1947–
     Clara Barton : "face danger, but never fear it" / Don Nardo.
          p. cm. — (Americans-the spirit of a nation)
          Summary: "Explores the life of Clara Barton and her tireless work as a teacher,
     a nurse on the frontlines of the Civil War, and her creation of the American Red
     Cross"—Provided by publisher.
     Includes bibliographical references and index.
     ISBN-13: 978-0-7660-3024-4
     ISBN-10: 0-7660-3024-5
          1. Barton, Clara, 1821–1912—Juvenile literature. 2. American Red Cross—
     Biography—Juvenile literature. 3. Nurses—United States—Biography—Juvenile
     literature. I. Title.
     HV569.B3N37 2008
     361.7'634092—dc22
     [B]
                                                           2007023378
Printed in the United States of America

10 9 8 7 6 5 4 3 2 1

To Our Readers:
We have done our best to make sure all Internet Addresses in this book were active
and appropriate when we went to press. However, the author and the publisher have
no control over and assume no liability for the material available on those Internet
sites or on other Web sites they may link to. Any comments or suggestions can be sent
by e-mail to comments@enslow.com or to the address on the back cover.

Illustration Credits: American Red Cross, p. 91; Associated Press, pp. 19, 69, 79, 87,
113; Clara Barton Birthplace Museum, pp. 20, 22; Clara Barton National Historic
Site/National Park Service, pp. 18, 36; Enslow Publishers, Inc., p. 14, 84, 94; The
Granger Collection, New York, pp. 6, 32, 63, 72, 102; Library of Congress, pp. 3, 8,
11, 27, 39, 41, 42, 44, 49, 53, 57, 59, 67, 75, 77, 85, 89, 95, 100–101, 104, 106, 111;
National Archives and Records Administration, p. 16; Special Collections/University
Archives, Rutgers University Libraries, pp. 30, 38.

Cover Illustration: The Library of Congress.

CONTENTS

Clara Barton aided many wounded soldiers during her time in the Civil War.

An Angel on the Battlefield

Bullets tore through the upper story of the old farmhouse, while outside cannons roared on all sides. Mingling with the deafening roar were the cries of mangled and dying men. Every room on the house's ground floor was packed with wounded soldiers. A few sufferers were tended to by doctors. But the majority lay alone in twisted heaps, some unconscious, others awake, and many bleeding to death.

For most of these unfortunate men, the only comfort was a woman named Clara Barton. With seemingly boundless energy, and with no thought for her own safety, she hurried from man to man. One witness later recalled that she "toiled as few men could have done." She placed bandages on "wounds which might otherwise have proved fatal."[1] She also gave thirsty men water and closed

Smith's Barn was used as a hospital during the battle at Antietam in September 1862.

the eyes of the dead. Though grateful, many of the men were shocked to see a woman. They wondered how she had managed to join them in the midst of what seemed like hell on earth.

A Perilous Mission

Barton's journey to the bloody farmhouse began three days before, on September 14, 1862. She rode in a large horse-drawn wagon that crept along a series of dusty

Maryland roads. Part of a U.S. Army supply train, the wagon was carrying bandages, other medical supplies, and food. Up ahead marched the soldiers who would soon badly need these supplies. Some eighty-seven thousand troops commanded by Major General George B. McClellan were marching toward the town of Sharpsburg. There, McClellan intended to attack a large army under the leading Confederate general, Robert E. Lee. The year before, eleven southern states had seceded, or separated, from the country. They had formed a new nation, the Confederate States of America, or the Confederacy, which was now engaged in a bloody war with the United States.

Like everyone marching with McClellan, Barton knew that the battle at Sharpsburg would be dangerous. Clearly, many people on both sides would not survive. But she and her two assistants wanted to help as many soldiers as they could. One assistant was a professional driver who knew how to handle the six mules pulling the rig. The other was Cornelius Welles, a Baptist minister and former missionary hired by Barton to help with her mission.

That perilous mission had sprung from a bold proposal Barton had recently made to officials in the U.S War Department. Before this, American women had not been allowed to set foot on active battlefields. Yet Barton convinced them to let her accompany the troops into combat. She pointed out that there were not enough army doctors. And many soldiers simply bled to death before any doctor could reach them. She insisted that civilians, including women, were badly needed on the war front. Such dedicated individuals could bring the numerous wounded men essential supplies and keep many of them from dying.

At Antietam Creek

Clara Barton was an unusually outspoken and persuasive individual. So the officials accepted her arguments. They also gave her special passes that allowed her and her assistants to join army supply trains. However, she was frustrated by the fact that the supply wagons were typically far from the action. The line of McClellan's troops stretched for ten miles along Maryland's dirt roadways. And Barton's wagon was located near the rear of the column. She worried that she and her helpers would not be able to quickly reach those who needed them.

To remedy what she saw as an unacceptable situation, Barton made another bold move. At about 1 A.M. on September 16, 1862, while most of the troops were asleep, she woke up Welles and the driver. At her order, they quietly drove the wagon past the sleeping men.

It was difficult to see their way in the darkness, and a thick mist floating in the air made the trek even more difficult. But then the sun rose and evaporated the mist. All through the morning and afternoon, Barton and her companions pressed on toward the front lines. When the sun set that day, they joined up with a company of Union soldiers camped near a creek called Antietam. No one then realized that this unimposing little stream would lend its name to a tragic battle.

America's Bloodiest Day

Clara Barton's efforts to save lives in the Battle of Antietam (also called the Battle of Sharpsburg) made her more than a hero. She was also an eyewitness to a major historical event. The battle was one of the largest and most complex fought during the American Civil War. More Americans died at Antietam on September 17, 1862, than on any other day in history.[2] The Union forces commanded by George B. McClellan lost 2,108 dead. The Confederates, led by Robert E. Lee, suffered 1,546 killed. The combined American death toll of 3,654 is higher than that of the Japanese attack on Pearl Harbor in 1941. The Antietam death toll also exceeds American losses in the D-Day invasion of France in 1944 and the September 11 attacks in New York City in 2001.

To the Sounds of the Guns

The conflict began early the next morning. At about 3 A.M., Barton and her assistants were jolted awake by the sound of gunfire. Leaving the men to guard the wagon, she climbed a nearby hill to see what was happening. She had no sooner reached the summit when cannons began roaring all around her. The ground trembled from the vibrations unleashed by the deadly barrage.

Barton realized that she must follow the sounds of the guns. That way she would be available to wounded men when they needed her most. Racing back to the wagon, she told the driver to take them toward Sharpsburg. As dawn broke, it was clear that the heart of the fight was developing in some fields southeast of the town. Barton's party followed a line of Union soldiers as they rushed toward the battle lines. Soon she saw wounded men staggering from a cornfield. She ordered the wagon to plunge into the tall stalks.

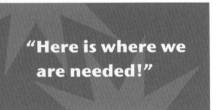

"Here is where we are needed!"

Barton and her helpers reached the farmhouse surrounded by the cornfield. Some three hundred wounded men were already lying around the structure and a nearby barn. "Here is where we are needed!" she shouted over the roar of gunfire.[3] As bullets and shells exploded around them, the three relief workers drove to the house. On the porch, an army surgeon, Dr. James Dunn, struggled to aid the wounded.

When the doctor saw Clara Barton approaching, his face lit up with a mixture of amazement and joy. The two had met briefly a few months before, when she had helped him at an army hospital. Stepping from the porch he declared, "God has indeed remembered us!" Then he told her how desperate the situation was:

> *We have nothing but our instruments, and the little chloroform [an anesthetic] we brought in our pockets. I have torn up the last sheets we could find in this house and have not a bandage, rag, lint or string. And all these wounded men [are] bleeding to death.*[4]

Death in an Instant

Barton told Dunn that there were bandages and other supplies in her wagon. Then she and her companions got right to work. For a while, she tended to the dozens of wounded men inside the house. Then she made her way to the barn, where more bleeding soldiers huddled.

Barton heard bullets fired from the nearby battlefield strike both the barn and house on a regular basis. But at first she paid little attention to the deadly barrage. She did not fully appreciate the danger until she tried crossing from the barn back to the house. One badly wounded young man in the yard saw her and begged for some water. She fetched some from a bucket beside a nearby well and ran back to him. Raising his head, she tried to pour some water into his mouth. Suddenly, she felt the sleeve on her right arm flutter just as the soldier's body lurched from her grasp.

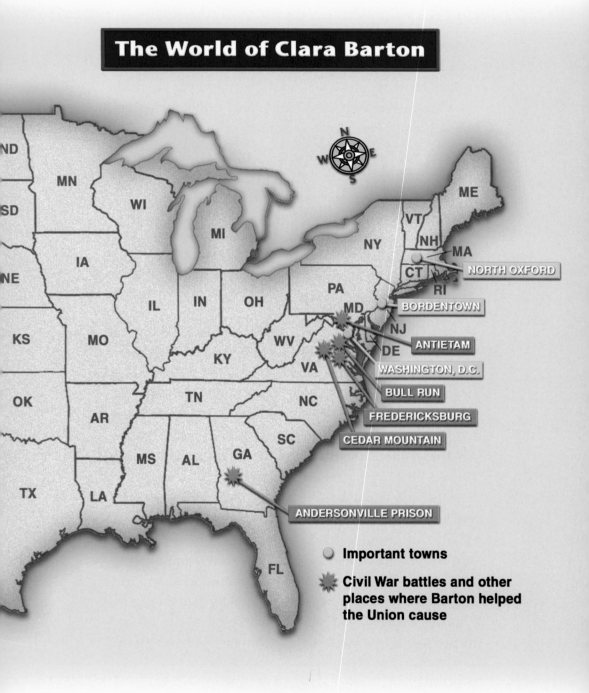

The World of Clara Barton

- **Important towns**
- **Civil War battles and other places where Barton helped the Union cause**

She realized that a bullet had passed straight through her sleeve and into the wounded man. In an instant, he was dead.

Although she was horrified by the event, Barton did not allow herself to be overwhelmed by what had just happened. She knew that the rest of the men badly needed her help. At all costs, she must remain calm and keep working. It was now clear to her that the remaining men in the yard had to be moved out of harm's way. So she and Welles hastily organized the few soldiers who were still able to walk. And together they began dragging the more seriously wounded men into the barn.

Extraordinary Courage Under Fire

A few minutes later, a soldier approached Clara Barton near the barn door. A bullet was embedded in his cheek, he told her. It would be hours before the doctors could attend to such a minor wound. In the meantime, he said, the pain was nearly unbearable. So could she remove the bullet? At first she refused, saying she was worried she would hurt him. "You can't hurt me," he assured her. "I can endure any pain your hands can create."[5] Gathering her nerve, Barton took out her pocketknife. And while another wounded man held the soldier's head still, she cut the bullet out, then cleaned and dressed the wound.

Barton continued to aid the wounded all day without a break. By nightfall, her face was covered with dirt and soot and her hair was all tangled. The battle was over, and by September 19, Lee had retreated from

Gruesome Battlefield Amputations

When Clara Baron and her assistants arrived at the farmhouse in the cornfield near Sharpsburg, they beheld a ghastly scene. Dr. James Dunn, an army surgeon, and a handful of assistants were feverishly treating wounded men.

Many of the wounds required that a limb be amputated. At the time, battlefield amputations were gruesome affairs. Often there was no anesthetic for the patient. In such cases, someone placed a thick piece of leather between the patient's teeth so he could bite down on it while he screamed. Working as quickly as possible, the doctor used a razor-sharp knife to slice through the flesh. Then he applied a saw to the bone and employed pliers to snip off jagged ends of bone. The amputated limb was often thrown into a growing pile of such body parts.

Despite the doctors' best efforts, a high percentage of battlefield amputees died of fever or infection within a few days.

A battlefield surgeon performs an amputation in 1863.

Sharpsburg. In his wake, some twelve thousand four hundred Union soldiers and more than ten thousand three hundred Confederate soldiers were dead, wounded, or missing in what would become known as the Battle of Antietam. In a letter to his wife, Dunn told about the human catastrophe he had witnessed. But there was one bright spot in all the chaos and misery, he wrote. He recalled Clara Barton's selflessness and the extraordinary courage she had shown under fire. He called her "the true hero of the age, the angel of the battlefield."[6]

But Barton did not think of herself as a hero. In her view, she was only fulfilling a need. Her country badly needed people to care for wounded and sick people during wars and other major emergencies. She could not then foresee that she would one day almost single-handedly create a national organization dedicated to that noble purpose.

Chapter 2

Learning the Value of Selflessness

Clara Barton's parents and siblings thought her entry into the world was a special Christmas present. That is because she was born on December 25, Christmas Day, in 1821. Clarissa Harlowe Barton was the youngest of Stephen and Sarah Stone Barton's five children. The others—Dorothy, Sally, Stephen, and David—were all delighted with the new arrival. They enjoyed playing with her, rocking her to sleep, and assigning her pet names. For a while these included "Tot," "Tabatha," "Baby," and "Clary." Eventually everyone got used to a simple abbreviation of Clarissa—Clara, which means "light."

A House Full of Tutors

Most of all, the other members of the family enjoyed teaching young Clara about life and the wide world that existed beyond their little town. The quaint hamlet of North Oxford was located in a heavily wooded area of south-central Massachusetts. There, Stephen Barton, a former soldier, had established himself as a successful farmer and mill owner. The nearest large town,

The Clara Barton birthplace and museum is in North Oxford, Massachusetts. The eleven-room farmhouse is filled with memorabilia of the founder of the American Red Cross.

Sarah Barton

Promoting Women's Rights

Clara Barton often surprised and amazed people by tackling jobs traditionally done by men. Her belief that women can do anything men do came first from her mother. Sarah Barton was a staunch proponent of women's rights. And she was not shy about voicing her opinions on the matter. Clara later said that her mother supported "the full right of women to all privileges and positions which nature and justice accord her."[1]

Worcester, was about eight miles to the north. And the state's largest city, Boston, was almost fifty miles away to the northeast.

Though they lived in a remote area, the Bartons were not isolated from social and political events. Stephen Barton was active in both local and state politics. In North Oxford, he served as a selectman and ran the town meetings. He also served as a representative to the state legislature, called the Massachusetts General Court.

In addition, Clara's father was a member of the local school board. He believed strongly in the value of education, for both men and women. In his view, neither North Oxford, nor Massachusetts, nor America could achieve progress and prosperity without everyone going to school. His wife agreed and they passed on their strong concerns about education to the children. Clara's oldest sister, Dorothy, nicknamed Dolly, was already a seventeen-year-old teacher at Oxford's small schoolhouse when Clara was born. Her brother Stephen, then fifteen, also later became a teacher.

Thus, Clara Barton grew up with what amounted to several personal tutors. Dolly taught her to write and spell. By age four, Clara could correctly spell many three- and four-syllable words. Meanwhile, Stephen, a math whiz, taught Clara arithmetic. Sally taught her geography, including the location of several European nations that Clara would one day visit. And David instructed his youngest sister in riding horses and the proper way to throw a ball. Finally, from her mother

Stephen Barton

A Proud Old Soldier

Throughout her life, Clara Barton expressed a keen interest in soldiers and soldiering. In large part this came from hearing about her father's military exploits as a young man.

Born in 1774, two years before the birth of the United States, Stephen Barton had fought under the command of former Revolutionary War general "Mad Anthony" Wayne in the 1790s. It was then that Wayne's forces defeated several American Indian tribes in the Ohio Valley.

Even after settling down to raise a family in Massachusetts, Barton retained his military connections and served as a captain in the local militia. His famous daughter later recalled: "His soldier habits and tastes never left him."[2] To his dying day, she said, he loved telling war stories and spouting military jargon.

Clara learned to sew, cook, garden, and keep a clean, organized house.

Good and Bad School Experiences

Not surprisingly, all this attention to learning made Clara an eager and hard-working student when she began attending school. Beginning around age four, she attended a series of local schools. Most were small, with one or two classrooms in which children of various ages mingled. Clara long retained pleasant memories of one of her teachers, Richard Stone. Among other things, he expanded her fascination for geography, which her sister Sally had kindled.

Clara later recalled her excitement at learning to read world maps: "[I] persisted in waking my poor drowsy sister in the cold winter mornings to sit up in bed and by the light of a tallow candle, help to find mountains, rivers, counties, oceans, [and] lakes."[3]

Stone also imparted to the young Clara a number of patriotic and moral ideas and some sober realities about life. One of these realities that remained with her always was that "death is the only thing certain in the world." Stone also reinforced a sense of discipline that Clara's parents had instilled in her. Learning is the key to understanding and happiness, he advised, and "knowledge is gained only by constant study."[4]

> **"Death is the only thing certain in the world."**
>
> —Richard Stone, Clara Barton's teacher

Although Clara's early school experiences revealed her to be an excellent student, she did not always feel that she fit in. She was sometimes painfully shy around other students. So she often kept to herself. When Clara was nine, her parents decided that the way to cure this problem was to send their youngest daughter away to boarding school. Each Monday morning, Clara boarded a stagecoach, which took her to school in a nearby town. She would remain there until Friday afternoon, then return home on the weekend. The theory was that being on her own for five days a week would force the young girl to develop social skills and overcome her shyness.

This plan quickly backfired, however, because Clara was lonely and miserable at the boarding school. She felt nervous around so many strange people. And she was often the butt of jokes among several of her classmates. One day a girl pretended that Clara had borrowed a bracelet from her. When the girl demanded it back, Clara was so upset that she fainted. Another embarrassing moment occurred in class. Clara badly mispronounced the name of an Egyptian king and the other students laughed at her. She ran from the room and refused to return. Fortunately for her, her father decided that sending her to the boarding school had been a mistake and brought her home.

Enjoying Both Work and Play

Clara was clearly happy to be back in North Oxford on a full-time basis. Her mood improved even more a few months later when the family moved to a larger house in the same town. One of her uncles had recently died. The Bartons now took in his six children—three boys and three girls, cousins who were all near Clara's age. The children enjoyed exploring the many acres of woods that surrounded the house. Also, as Clara later wrote, there were "three temptingly great barns" on the property. "Was there ever a better opportunity for hide-and-seek, for jumping and climbing?" she remembered fondly.[5]

Though Clara and her cousins played when they could, they also had chores to do. Yet ten-year-old Clara rarely thought of her own chores as work. Her main duty was to look after the many animals the family kept. She cared for, as well as milked, the cows. And she fed and tended the ducks, lambs, dogs, and cats that had the run of the farm. Clara viewed all of these creatures as her pets and actually looked forward to the hours she spent with them.

"Will you teach me to paint, sir?"

Many of Clara's other hours were devoted to learning, not only at school, but also from various life situations that arose. She later recalled, for example, how she learned to paint. Her parents had hired a professional painter to decorate several rooms in the house. The young girl was fascinated with his skills. Gathering her courage one day, she asked him, "Will you teach me to paint, sir?"

He answered, "With pleasure, little lady, if mama is willing. I should very much like your assistance."

Mrs. Barton gave her consent. Clara later wrote:

I was taught how to hold my brushes, to take care of them, allowed to help grind my paints, shown how to mix and blend them, how to make putty and use it, to prepare oils and dryings . . . was taught to trim [wall]paper neatly, [and] to match and help to hang it. . . . [I] even varnished the kitchen chairs to the entire satisfaction of my mother, which was triumph enough for one little girl.[6]

Some Family Tragedies

However, not all of Clara Barton's childhood memories were as fond as those involving her playmates, pets, and painter friend. She also looked back on some family tragedies. These showed her that life can sometimes be painful, even cruel, and taught her how to face misfortune with courage.

One of these tragedies involved Clara's oldest sister, Dolly, to whom she was particularly close. At some point in the 1820s, Dolly had a mental breakdown. The exact nature of her condition is unknown, but the symptoms included frequent emotional outbursts and violent episodes. In one incident, she attacked her sister-in-law with an ax. Unfortunately for all involved, mental illness was poorly understood in those days and existing care was difficult to obtain. The best the Bartons could do was to lock Dolly in her bedroom most of the time. Everyone in the family learned to deal with the confined young women's frequent screams and demands to be released from confinement. Dolly died in 1846, at age forty-two. Clara, twenty-five at the time, was forever haunted by her sister's plight.

Clara's brother, David, was involved in a distressing incident. When she was eleven, he and some local men were building a barn. David was working on the roof when the wooden plank on which he was standing suddenly gave way, causing him to fall. Though he managed to land on his feet, he soon developed a fever, severe headaches, and other debilitating symptoms. The local doctors were at a loss to identify what was

Clara helped nurse her brother David back to health.

wrong with David, who became bedridden. So they fell back on a common medical treatment of that era called "bleeding." It consisted of removing supposedly "bad blood" from a person's body in hopes of affecting a cure. To draw out the blood, one placed leeches on the patient's skin.

Clara volunteered to care for David and draw his blood on a regular basis. She later recalled:

> *My little hands became schooled to the handling of the great, loathsome, crawling leeches, which were at first [like] so many snakes to me, and no fingers could so painlessly dress the angry blisters. Thus it came about that I was the accepted and acknowledged nurse of a man almost too ill to recover.*[7]

David did finally recover, but not as a result of the bleeding sessions. After he had suffered for almost two years, a new doctor prescribed eating a healthier diet and sitting in a steam room for extended periods. This approach eliminated his symptoms.

Mature Beyond Her Years

What most impressed everyone, family members and doctors alike, was the extreme dedication shown by David's sister Clara. She had remained almost constantly at his side for the entire two years. Throughout the ordeal, she had shown a level of maturity and compassion far beyond her years. Perhaps this was partly the result of growing up among many educated, caring individuals. Yet Clara's own sharp intelligence and strong inner compulsion to aid those in need also played a part.

Whatever factors may have shaped the young Clara Barton, she learned the value of selflessness. This noble trait would become a permanent part of her character. It would guide her through virtually all of her adult endeavors. The first of these was teaching, which she began while still a teenager. At the time, she had no way of knowing that it would be only one of a long series of professional and humanitarian adventures.

Chapter 3

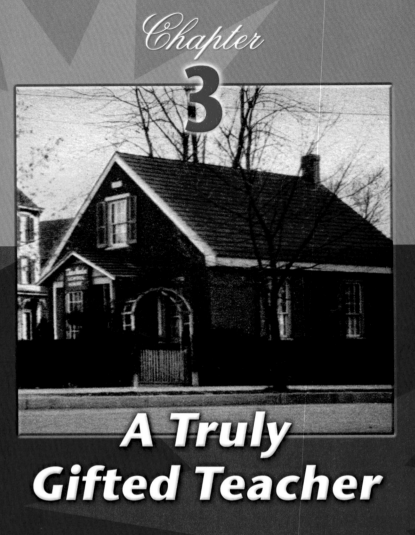

A Truly Gifted Teacher

As it turned out, Clara Barton was a very good educator. One of her cousins, Elvira Stone, later said that she "took to teaching as natural as could be."[1] Indeed, in a teaching career that spanned fifteen years, Barton won the respect and admiration of her students, their parents, and school officials alike. And in the process, she changed countless lives for the better.

Mixing Kindness with Firmness

Even before entering the formal setting of a school, Barton displayed her natural teaching abilities. When she was only fourteen, she felt the urge to help some of North Oxford's poorest families. She often spent long hours nursing sick mothers or sick children back to health. She also helped the same children keep up with their schoolwork. She became in a very real way their tutor. And without realizing it, she gained valuable teaching experience that would serve her well later.

Barton acquired her first job as a formal classroom teacher in May 1839, when she was seventeen. At the time, becoming a teacher did not require a college-level education. In Massachusetts and most other states, the person applied to the local school board and took a proficiency test. In Clara Barton's case, a local judge, lawyer, and minister gave her a brief verbal exam and were satisfied that she was educated enough to teach.

The first school Barton took charge of was District School No. 9 in North Oxford. It was a rundown one-room structure attended by students of widely varying ages. Some were only a year or two younger than Barton and a few had even been her playmates. At first this seemed to present something of an awkward situation. After all, Barton later quipped, "We had all been children together."[2]

Yet the young woman quickly overcame this potential obstacle, establishing herself as a mature and respected authority figure. Moreover, the manner in which she did this impressed both the students and

A nineteenth-century schoolhouse usually consisted of a single room lined with benches. In colder areas, there was also a stove to heat the school.

school board. It was common in those days for teachers to employ corporal (physical) punishment to discipline their students. A child who misbehaved might receive one or more painful whacks of a ruler or hickory switch. But Barton firmly rejected this approach. One of her students later recalled, "I remember you walking about with your ruler in your hand, [but] I don't remember that you ever punished anyone. You used your ruler for other purposes."[3]

Clara Barton's approach to discipline was a mixture of kindness, firmness, and trust. When she encountered an unruly or undisciplined student, she remained calm. Speaking to the child in private, she took him or her into her confidence. Often she gave the student what seemed like an important responsibility or job to fulfill. That way, she and the child quickly became loyal allies.

One such success story involved a large, poorly behaved boy named Hart Bodine. Before Barton arrived at the school, Hart had a reputation for being a bully and rule-breaker. But on the first day of school, his mother later recalled, the new teacher immediately threw him off-guard. Barton fearlessly and firmly confronted him. She told him that she badly needed him to behave and help her adjust to her new job. She also had him dispose of the switches the former teacher had used to punish him. "She had him carry them outdoors and break them into small bits," Mrs. Bodine said. Then she "tenderly took him by the hand, assuring him she would never need them, for he was one of her big boys and she could depend on him to help keep order in the school, he was simply overwhelmed," and became one of the best behaved students in the school.[4]

A Good Reputation

Barton rapidly gained a reputation for her ability to win over potentially troublesome students. In fact, at the close of the first term, the members of the school board gave her an award for having the best-disciplined classroom in the district. That made her much in demand as a teacher. And teaching offers began to come from other towns. In 1840, she agreed to teach in the village of Charlton, just west of North Oxford.

The school in Charlton had fifty students of varying ages. For teaching them and maintaining order and discipline in the building, Barton was paid about two dollars a week. This was considerably less than what male teachers made at the time for similar jobs. Most people in that era viewed it as the natural way of things for women to be treated as second-class citizens. Not only did they make less money than men, women were not allowed to vote or hold public office.

> **"I shall never do a man's work for less than a man's pay."**

At first, Clara Barton was content to accept her smaller teaching salary. But she eventually changed her mind. Over time, she taught in many different schools in North Oxford and neighboring towns. And she built up a great reputation that helped her get the wage she wanted from her bosses. Eventually she told them, "I may sometimes be willing to teach for nothing. But if paid at all, I shall never do a man's work for less than a man's pay."[5] In a move that was quite unheard of at the time, the North Oxford school board agreed to this demand.

Her Busy Private Life

During her early years as a teacher, Barton was also busy outside of school. She often helped with the bookkeeping of a local mill business run by her brothers. She also did chores and errands for North Oxford's Universalist Church. These activities included running charity drives, collecting old clothes to give to the poor, and cleaning the church's windows.

Despite her involvement with the church, however, Clara Barton was not a devoutly religious person. It appears that she believed in some form of higher power. But she was not convinced that this higher power cared much about humanity. The evidence for this, in her mind, was the extreme poverty and suffering she had already witnessed in her young life. Thus, her church activities were for the most part a way to help her friends and community.

Another distraction from Barton's classroom duties consisted of the attentions of three young men who admired and courted her. One was one of her cousins. Another lived in a local North Oxford boarding house in which she sometimes stayed. The third man has never been identified. For some unknown reason, she never mentioned his name in her writings. What is more certain is that she ended up turning down the marriage proposals from all three suitors. Her exact reasons are unclear. But it is likely that she felt too devoted to her work to find time for a husband and family. One of her best friends during these years, Fanny Vassall, later suggested: "Clara Barton was herself so much stronger a character than any of the men who [loved] her that I do not think she was ever seriously tempted to marry any of them."[6]

Fighting for Public Education

In fact, Barton was so dedicated to teaching that she spent much of her spare time reading. She felt that the more she learned, the more knowledge she could impart

Clara Barton attended Clinton Liberal Institute in 1850.

to her students. Another way she tried to improve her teaching skills was through higher education. In 1850, after more than ten years as a professional educator, she took a leave of absence. She then enrolled in a highly reputable teacher's college—Clinton Liberal Institute, in Clinton, New York.

While studying at the Liberal Institute, Barton became close friends with a younger classmate, Mary Norton. In 1851, the two took a short vacation to Norton's hometown of Hightstown, New Jersey. And while there, Barton learned that a school in nearby Bordentown badly needed a teacher. What appealed most to her was that the school was known for having serious discipline problems. She met with the Bordentown school superintendent, who was impressed and offered her a job.

Like other schools in New Jersey at the time, the Cedarville School, where Barton taught, was a subscription school. This was a fancy way of saying a private school. The parents of the students provided the money to pay the teachers and buy books and other supplies. This did not bother Barton at first. But after a while she noticed that hundreds of children from the town's poorer families never attended school. Plainly, their parents could not afford the tuition. One day she approached a boy who was hanging around a street corner and asked why he was not in school. "Lady, there is no school for us," he replied.[7]

Distraught at this situation, Barton decided that something must be done. She went to her boss and asked why there were no publicly funded schools.

He said most people thought that such schools would be a waste of money. The poor children were poorly motivated to learn, he claimed, and would not attend school on a regular basis. But Barton disagreed. She offered to teach for several months without pay if the school board would find a building and open a public school.

Early in 1852, Clara Barton opened the new school, the first successful free public school in New Jersey. On the first day, only six students showed up at the little two-room building. But within five weeks, some two hundred children were regularly attending. By the end of the first school year, that number had grown to more than six hundred. And the town had to provide a building with enough classrooms to fit all the local students who wanted to receive an education.

This postcard from the 1920s shows the first public school in New Jersey, opened by Clara Barton in Bordentown in 1852.

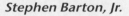

Stephen Barton, Jr.

Some Brotherly Support

During the years she taught school in Bordentown, New Jersey, Clara Barton often exchanged letters with family members back in Massachusetts. She was particularly close to her brother Stephen. And he tried to console her during her troubles with the Bordentown school board during the 1853–1854 school year. In letters written in February 1854, he told her:

> *You have done much to establish the system of free schools in the city and in so doing have done an infinite amount of good to the rising generations. . . . I am sorry that things have taken such a turn in the public schools and think it must be unpleasant to you after you have done so much [for] them to feel that you cannot with . . . respect to yourself continue to assist them.*[8]

Sudden Disappointment

In one respect, the school's great success was a triumph for Barton. She had proved that public education was the wave of the future in New Jersey and elsewhere. But her feelings of pride and elation were soon tempered by the social realities of the day. When the new school building opened in 1853, she found herself once more being treated poorly because she was a woman. The men on the school board decided that a woman would not be capable of running so large a facility. Even though her ideas and hard work had made the school possible, the school board hired a man to run it. Even worse, the board members paid him twice as much as Barton.

This time, Barton's protests about fairness and equal pay for equal work fell on deaf ears. The school board refused to listen to her. As months passed, she became increasingly frustrated and unhappy. Early in 1854, Barton resigned from the school. She decided to move to nearby Washington, D.C., to rest for a while and think about her future. She did not realize at the time that she would never teach again. Nor did she foresee the series of dramatic turns her life would take in the next two decades.

4

Coming to the Aid of Her Country

Clara Barton later gave a variety of reasons for her decision to go to Washington, D.C. One was health-related. During the stressful months leading up to her departure from Bordentown, New Jersey, she had lost her voice. A common folk belief at the time was the farther south one went, the milder and healthier the air. "I wanted the mild air for my throat," she later wrote.[1] Another reason she

Clara Barton

gave for the move to Washington was her interest in politics. And still another was her desire to take advantage of the large number of books stored at the Library of Congress.

Whatever her motives for settling in the nation's capital, Barton took a room in a respectable boarding house. There, she rested and read many books. These included historical and political texts as well as guides to mastering French. She also frequently went to the Capitol building and sat in the balconies of the Senate and House chambers. She found it both instructive and entertaining to listen to the lively debates among national legislators. Whatever the activities that filled her days, she relished the fact that she had no pressing duties or plans. "I enjoyed my quiet, almost friendless and unknown life," she later recalled.[2]

The Highest Paid Woman in Washington

For Barton, the difference between "almost friendless" and friendless was, in a sense, the key that opened the door to the rest of her life. She did strike up a friendship with a man she saw repeatedly during her visits to the Capitol. He was Alexander DeWitt, the congressman from her home district in Massachusetts. As it turned out, he was also a distant cousin.

DeWitt was immediately taken with the young woman's intelligence and earnest and pleasant manner. He knew she needed to find a job to support herself in the bustling city. He suggested she apply for a position

Alexander DeWitt suggested that Clara Barton apply for a job at the U.S. Patent Office.

at the U.S. Patent Office. DeWitt introduced her to the director of the Patent Office, Charles Mason. Mason was also impressed with Barton and offered her a part-time job copying documents. (Because no copy machines existed then, all such work had to be done by hand.) She began the new job in July 1854. Paid by the number of words she copied, reportedly she earned eight cents for every hundred words.

Soon, however, Mason made Barton a full-time clerk. That made her the first woman to draw a regular salary from the government in her own name.[3] (Three other women working in the same office were substituting for their disabled husbands; so their paychecks were in their husbands' names.) Moreover, Mason broke with precedent and paid Barton the same as he would pay a man in the job—$1,400 a year. In comparison, female bookkeepers then earned $500 per year, female teachers $250 per year, and female store clerks $156 per year.[4] Incredibly, only a few months after arriving in Washington, Clara Barton was the highest-paid woman in the city.

But some of the men in the patent office felt threatened by the new arrival. They thought that allowing women such equality was unnatural and dangerous. So they sexually harassed her, calling her nasty names, in hopes of forcing her to quit. But she refused to be intimidated. Also, Mason came to her aid. He told one harasser either to offer concrete proof that she was bad and undeserving or quit his own position. The man backed down, and the harassment stopped.

Helping Washington's Defenders

Barton's experiences at the Patent Office taught her a number of useful lessons. One was that having friends in high places could open doors, not only for herself but also for any people or groups she might decide to help. So she made a point of getting to know as many influential and powerful people as she could. One was a senator from Massachusetts, Henry Wilson.

The first great cause of Barton's life materialized in 1861. On April 12, troops from South Carolina attacked a federal facility in that state, Fort Sumter. South Carolina had seceded from the United States in December of the preceding year, followed by six other states. And soon after the attack on Fort Sumter, four more southern states left the Union, making eleven in all. These events marked the beginning of the American Civil War.

Clara Barton was appalled to see her country breaking up. And she thought it was equally terrible that Americans would choose to fight other Americans. Yet she was not completely against the idea of using physical force when necessary. In fact, she told a friend that she herself would be perfectly willing to fight, if necessary, to save the capital and the Union. If the Confederates marched on Washington, she said, let them come. "And when there is no longer a soldier's arm to raise the Stars and Stripes above our Capitol, may God give strength to mine!"[5] Thus, though later she did at times help wounded Confederate soldiers, her sentiments were clearly with the North. "I am a plain Northern Union woman," she declared, "honest in my feelings . . . desiring only the good of all."[6]

> "When there is no longer a soldier's arm to raise the Stars and Stripes above our Capitol, may God give strength to mine!"

Barton began to worry less that the Confederates might attack Washington soon. President Abraham Lincoln, who took office on March 4, 1861, called for a volunteer army to defend the capital. Eventually, as many as seventy-five thousand men from various northern states responded. But Barton was dismayed to see that most of these troops had no place to stay. Some camped out in tents wherever they could find open spaces. In desperation, government officials allowed some of them to sleep in the Senate chamber in the Capitol building.

The problem was that many of the soldiers had arrived with only whatever supplies they could carry. "They have nothing but their heavy woolen clothes," Barton wrote to a friend. "And many of them [lack] even a pocket handkerchief." The sad fact was that government officials were too ill-prepared and disorganized to meet the soldiers' daily needs. So Barton took it upon herself to render aid. She organized some local women and

> *[we] emptied our pockets and came home to tear up old sheets for towels and handkerchiefs, and have filled a large box with all manner of serving utensils, thread, needles, thimbles, scissors, pins, buttons, strings, salves, tallow, etc.*[7]

Barton also organized a letter-writing campaign to people in Massachusetts. She asked that they send as many supplies as they could for the troops in Washington. Tons of blankets, clothing, canned foods, and medical supplies quickly arrived and filled Barton's rented room from floor to ceiling. Overwhelmed, she went to the army quartermaster, Major D. H. Rucker. She requested that he find a warehouse to store the incoming goods, which he did. In the months that followed, hundreds of tons of supplies poured into that depot.

Meanwhile, when she could find the time, Barton visited with the troops living in the Senate chamber. They were delighted when she read them the latest newspaper stories while sitting in the chair normally used by the president of the Senate.

The Gruesome Realities of War

In the months that followed, Clara Barton continued to be dismayed at the government's inefficiency in supplying its fighting men. She was also shocked at the poor care given to wounded soldiers. This became clear to her on July 21, 1861. In the first major land battle of the war, the Confederates soundly defeated a Union

A Sad Letter Home

Many of Barton's personal feelings about and reactions to the Civil War are preserved in letters she wrote to family members. In a letter written on July 26, 1861, to her father, Barton describes her shock and sadness over the North's defeat at Bull Run: "This has been a hard day to witness—sad, painful and mortifying. . . . We are defeated, the worst and sorest of defeats. . . . how gladly would I close my eyes to it if I could."[8]

The First Battle of Bull Run occurred on July 21, 1861.

army at Bull Run, in northern Virginia. The North lost 460 killed and 1,124 wounded. And Barton learned that almost no preparations had been made to care for large numbers of wounded men. There were not nearly enough medical supplies for them. Nor was there enough food.

Even worse, Barton realized the terrible truth that many of the men died simply because they had not received medical treatment in a timely manner. Hundreds lay around for many hours or even a couple of days with no bandages for their wounds. So men who might well have recovered simply bled to death.

In fact, Barton was suddenly coming to grips with some of the truly gruesome realities of warfare in that era. She later learned that, in large part because of lack of timely medical attention, 87 percent of soldiers with deep abdominal wounds died. Also, 63 percent of those with chest wounds perished. And 60 percent of men with skull wounds met the same fate. In addition, fully 33 percent of troops with shoulder wounds died, often from infection. Worse still, inadequate medical care caused otherwise minor wounds to require amputation of feet, hands, arms, and legs. And more than half of the soldiers who endured amputations at the thigh or knee joint died within a few days or weeks.[9]

A Personal Victory

Barton learned that the army simply did not have enough doctors to care for large numbers of wounded men quickly and effectively. So there was clearly a desperate need for volunteers to help out in battle situations. They could bring the troops the supplies they required. The volunteers could also care for wounded soldiers, saving many lives.

In Clara Barton's mind, it did not matter whether these volunteers were men or women. But most people, including military officials, frowned on the idea of allowing women near ongoing battles. The military front was "no place for a lady," Major D. H. Rucker told Barton when she asked for permission to travel with the army.

"I have no fear of the battlefield," she retorted.

"Have you got a father or brother there?" he asked.

The Horrors of War

The extreme need for battlefield nurses like Clara Barton in the Civil War is illustrated by this eyewitness account. A nurse wrote it on a Northern army hospital ship early in the conflict.

> *There were eight hundred [wounded men] on board. Passageways, state-rooms, floors from the dark and [stinking] hold to the hurricane deck, were all more than filled; some [men lay] on mattresses, some on blankets, others on straw; some [were] in the death-struggle, others nearing it, [and] some already beyond human sympathy and help . . . and all [were] hungry and thirsty.*[10]

"No," she answered. "I have some things I want to take to the soldiers. But I need wagons and a pass to get them there."[11]

At first, Rucker was reluctant to grant Barton's unusual demands. But she refused to back down. So he gave in and wrote her the passes she needed to get to the front. He also gave her a wagon and a driver. Perhaps he did so partly because he was moved by her selflessness and courage. But surely he was also motivated by a real concern for the soldiers. If this stubborn, gutsy woman was willing to risk her life to help them, who was he to stand in her way?

As she left Rucker's office, the precious passes in hand, Clara Barton was pleased. She had won an important concession—the right of a woman to help out during the conflict's major battles. But she could not waste time and energy celebrating her personal victory. Soldiers were already dying needlessly, she told herself, and she was determined to save as many of them as she could.

Into the Heat of Battle

Clara Barton's acquisition of battlefield passes from a high army official marked a turning point in the conduct of war in America. Before, all female nurses who aided wounded soldiers belonged to a few small humanitarian organizations. Notable was the U.S. Sanitary Commission, run by Henry Bellows and Dorothea Dix. Its members collected supplies for the soldiers and staffed military hospitals. Other similar groups were the Soldiers Aid Society and the Christian Commission. However, none of these organizations allowed women to work at the front. Moreover, no army doctors had ever requested the services of female nurses behind the battle lines.

Barton and her female assistants were therefore pioneers of a sort. The first woman she asked to help her was Anna Carver, who had already spent several months tending to wounded soldiers in Washington, D.C. Among the other female nurses who later helped Clara Barton were Almira Fales, Ada Morrell, and Lydie Haskell.

Not one to discriminate, Barton also allowed men to help her. Her most trustworthy male assistant was a Baptist minister, Cornelius Welles. Welles possessed several qualities that Clara Barton admired. For one thing, he was deeply devoted to aiding ill, wounded, and needy people, no matter what their situation. Also, unlike most men, Welles was perfectly willing to take orders from a woman. That, Barton foresaw, would be absolutely essential in their working relationship. From the start, she insisted on being in complete charge of her battlefield-relief unit.

Heading for the Front

With Anna Carver and Cornelius Welles on her team, Barton wasted no time in leading that unit toward the front. On August 2, 1862, the three struck out for Fredericksburg, Virginia, located about fifty miles southwest of the U.S. capital. Many Union troops were camped near that city. Rumors abounded that the

Confederates were massing for a large-scale attack. Barton correctly reasoned that the fastest way to get to the action would be by boat—south along the Potomac River. So she and her helpers loaded their supplies onto a government tugboat.

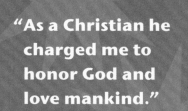

"As a Christian he charged me to honor God and love mankind."

Standing on deck and watching the changing scenery along the shore, Clara Barton considered the grim task ahead. Her thoughts also drifted to her family. A few months before, in March, her father had passed away at age eighty-seven. On his deathbed, Stephen Barton had given his complete support to his daughter's aspirations to follow the troops into battle. "I know soldiers," he had told her, "and they will respect you and your errand." Furthermore, she later recalled,

> *As a patriot he bade me serve my country with all I had [and] even [give] my life if need be. . . . He bade me seek and comfort the afflicted everywhere, and as a Christian he charged me to honor God and love mankind.*[1]

Barton also thought about her beloved brother Stephen. He had earlier moved his sawmill business to South Carolina. And when that state had seceded from the Union, she had urged him to return home rather than stay behind enemy lines. But he had refused to leave. Ever since, not a day had gone by that she did not worry about his safety.

Ordeal in Culpeper

Barton and her assistants arrived at Fredericksburg on August 4. They discovered that the rumors of an impending Confederate assault on that town had been inaccurate. However, the trip down the Potomac had not been a waste of time. New rumors circulated that a major battle was about to occur in the region of Culpeper, just west of Fredericksburg.

This time the rumors were true. The Battle of Cedar Mountain (also called Slaughter's Mountain) erupted just five days later, on August 9. It proved to be the first test for Barton and her crew under real combat conditions. Northern troops led by Major General Nathaniel Banks were defeated by Confederate troops commanded by Major General Thomas "Stonewall" Jackson. Union casualties numbered approximately fourteen hundred.

During the fighting, many of the wounded Union soldiers were taken to the courthouse and churches in Culpeper. Arriving on the scene, Barton found hundreds of wounded men lying around the courthouse grounds. No doctors tended to these men. Many of them were bleeding heavily and all were extremely hungry and thirsty.

It was not only the sad state of the injured soldiers that shocked Barton and her helpers. They also were horrified when they saw the filthy conditions in the makeshift hospitals army doctors had set up in the town. The hospital floors were covered with blood, dirt, and human waste. Large numbers of patients were in

A Zouave ambulance crew demonstrates the removal of wounded soldiers from the field. A Zouave was a type of Union soldier.

danger of becoming infected. But the doctors and their handful of attendants were too busy to clean up. So Barton and her helpers pitched in and cleaned the hospital as the doctors worked feverishly to save lives. During these same hours, Barton provided the conscious patients with food, water, and clean clothes, earning their heartfelt thanks.

It was in one of these makeshift hospitals that Clara Barton first met army surgeon James Dunn. At the time, he later remembered, he was wearing an old red shirt with the sleeves rolled up. And he was "covered with blood from head to foot."[2] Though surprised to see a woman behind the lines, Dunn was very grateful to have the extra help. He told her that he had run out of bandages and was greatly relieved when she produced a fresh supply from her wagon.

Barton spent two grueling days and nights in the Culpeper hospitals. Throughout the ordeal, she never got to sleep and ate only a few scraps of food. Before leaving town and tending to her own needs, she made one last stop. It was a house where some wounded Confederates, captured during the battle, were under guard. She was appalled that no one had yet seen to these men's needs. They assumed at first that she was a Virginian. They were dumbfounded when they learned that a northern woman had come to their aid of her own free will.

Piles of Bodies

Leaving Culpeper, Barton returned to Washington to take care of what she saw as some loose ends. The war threatened to drag on for months, perhaps even years. And it was clear that her services would be needed as long as battles were waged and soldiers were wounded. But she was still employed by the Patent Office. She thought it would be dishonest to continue drawing a salary for work she was not doing. But she was in for a surprise when she approached the agency's new director, D. P. Holloway. A staunch patriot, he thoroughly approved of her work with the soldiers. Moreover, he said it was unfair that she should perform such an important wartime job for free. After all, the troops and army doctors were all paid for their services. So he offered to keep paying part of her Patent Office wages for the remainder of the conflict. She later called the arrangement "a noble gift of a noble friend."[3]

Barton barely had time to thank her boss for his kind gesture when battlefield duty called once more. In the closing days of August 1862, an enormous battle raged at Bull Run. (The war's second engagement fought there, it is often called Second Bull Run or Second Manassas.) The Union lost, incurring heavy casualties—1,747 killed and 8,452 wounded.

Barton, this time accompanied by Almira Morrell, Ada Fales, and Cornelius Welles, arrived by train at Fairfax Station only a few hours after the last shots had

The Second battle of Bull Run left many wounded for Clara Barton and others to help.

been fired at Second Bull Run. They were greeted by a sight that made their hearts sink. More than three thousand wounded men sprawled beside the tracks. Many were screaming in pain, while others were crying out for food and water. Among the piles of writhing bodies, a handful of doctors toiled, amputating limbs and tossing them onto hideous heaps of severed flesh and bone.

It quickly became clear that Barton and her band of helpers were the only civilian volunteers on the scene. Getting right to work, they fed as many as men as they could. They also dressed hundreds of minor wounds and gave many of the soldiers clean clothes. In addition, they took the time to jot down the men's names. This would allow thousands of anxious families to know if their sons or brothers were alive or dead.

Narrow Escapes From Death

To call Barton's efforts at Second Bull Run tireless would be an understatement. In a period of more than four days, she managed to get by on only two hours of sleep. She and her assistants saved hundreds of lives that surely otherwise would have been lost.

Moreover, Barton showed the same determination and selflessness on many other Civil War battlefields in the years that followed. At Antietam, in September 1862, she and Dr. James Dunn crossed paths again. It was there that he called her the "angel of the battlefield," a phrase that would be forever associated with

A Touch of Kindness

In the wake of Second Bull Run, in late August 1862, Clara Barton fed the wounded troops and dressed their wounds. She also administered personal touches of kindness wherever she could.

One memorable case was that of a severely wounded young man named Hugh Johnson. A doctor told Barton that Johnson had no chance of survival and would be lucky to live a day or two. Feverish, Johnson called out for his sister, Mary. And for a little while, Barton became that woman. "Mary?" he asked. "Have you come? I knew you would come. Now I'm not afraid to die."[4] He ran his hand gently through Barton's hair, and she wrapped him in a shawl and rocked him to sleep.

The next day, she made sure that he was carrying a piece of paper with his name, her name, and other information. That way, if he died, before reaching his loved ones, his body could be properly identified. Hugh Johnson died two days later.

her name. It was also at Antietam that a Confederate bullet tore a hole in Barton's sleeve.

She narrowly escaped injury or death again at the Battle of Fredericksburg, in December 1862. In the midst of the fighting, a Northern officer was helping her ashore after she had crossed the Rappahannock River. Suddenly, an enemy shell exploded only a few feet away. Part of her skirt and a section of his coat were shredded, but both she and the officer escaped injury. (In a sad twist of fate, a few hours later she found him dead in the battlefield hospital.)

Perhaps not surprisingly, Barton's relentless heroics made her famous in the Union Army ranks. Many officers came to respect her, just as Rucker and Dunn had. Accordingly, they gave her higher status and authority. Thanks to D. H. Rucker, she eventually commanded seven supply wagons, each with six mules and a driver. Later, in May 1864, she was appointed superintendent of nurses for an entire division of the Union army. In this capacity, she organized and administered all military hospitals in the area of Petersburg, Virginia.

But as the months rolled by, it became clear to Barton that the war would eventually end and the North would win. Her services as a nurse would no longer be needed. So she began thinking about what she might do when peace came. She realized that she needed to do another job relating to the troops. In addition to dead and wounded, every battle resulted in numerous missing soldiers. Barton would make it her new mission to find them.

A Relentless Search for the Missing

Clara Barton's near obsession with finding missing soldiers stemmed partly from her interest in her brother Stephen's wartime experiences. In 1856, he had moved to North Carolina and established a lumber business. After some Union troops burned down his house, he began wandering through Confederate territory. And assuming he was a Confederate agent of some sort, Union troops arrested him and threw him into a military prison. Already ill when he entered the jail, Stephen grew steadily sicker due to the substandard living conditions.

Clara Barton eventually managed to convince the commander at Petersburg, General Benjamin Butler, that Stephen was not the enemy. And Butler agreed to transfer the sick man to Clara's care. She tried to nurse her brother back to health, but there was little she could do. He died in March 1865.

Barton reasoned that many of the Union soldiers listed as missing in action during the war suffered the same fate as her brother. Some of the missing were actually dead, she realized. Following large-scale battles, their bodies were often difficult to identify. And sometimes they were even misplaced and ended up in unmarked graves in the countryside. However, just as many missing soldiers had been thrown into enemy prison camps.

Barton felt it was imperative to locate all missing soldiers, wherever they might be. If they were alive, they could be reunited with their families. If they were dead, their families could achieve closure, peace of mind, and bury them with dignity.

A Problem of Enormous Scope

In fact, Barton was so eager to find missing soldiers that she did not wait until the end of the war. Confederate general Robert E. Lee surrendered at Appomattox, Virginia, on April 9, 1865. By this time, Barton was already heavily involved in the cause of missing troops. That involvement had begun with hundreds of letters she had received from the families of Union soldiers. Some thanked her for the aid she had rendered their fathers, sons, and brothers on the battlefield. But many others begged her to help them find relatives missing in action. A majority of these letters included detailed descriptions of the missing men. "People tell me the color of [the men's] hair & eyes," she later recalled, "as if I were expected to go about the country and search [for] them."[1]

Increasingly, Barton came to believe that someone did indeed need to launch such a search. The scope of the problem was truly enormous. By the end of the war, about one hundred seventy-two thousand Union war dead had been identified. Yet at least that many men were still missing. Surely some of them were dead and buried in unmarked graves. Others were likely alive and trying to make their way home.

Barton decided to devote herself to finding these men. Her initial plan had three parts. First, she would keep a close eye on the army's records of returning soldiers. These records were compiled in Annapolis, Maryland, where Barton took up temporary residence. Second, she would conduct searches of Confederate prison camps and look for lists of captured soldiers, as well as the graves and bodies of those prisoners who had died. Third, she would pass the information she had gathered to the families and friends of those missing.

Support From the President

To get her new project going, in February 1865 Barton established a private, unofficial missing person's bureau in Annapolis. It was called the Office of Correspondence with Friends of the Missing Men of the United States Army. Along with her sister, Sally Vassal, and a few friends, Barton read and answered the many letters that poured in. They also posted lists of missing men in the army barracks at Annapolis and constantly updated the lists.

It was clear, however, that the task Barton had undertaken was too big for a handful of people working on a tight budget. She and her staff needed the War Department's official lists of the dead. They also badly needed money to pay for postage, extra helpers, and trips to scattered prison camps. At first, Barton paid for much of this with her own funds and she quickly exhausted her savings account.

So Barton wrote to President Abraham Lincoln, hoping to get his backing for her operation. At the time, Lincoln was too busy to see her. However, Barton's friend, Senator Henry Wilson, offered to brief the president about her concerns. And on March 11, 1865, Lincoln issued her a letter of support. It stated:

> *To the friends of missing persons: Miss Clara Barton has kindly offered to search for the missing prisoners of War. Please address her at Annapolis, Maryland giving name, regiment, and company of any missing prisoner. A. Lincoln.*[2]

President Abraham Lincoln

Barton was extremely grateful for Lincoln's support. She still looked forward to meeting with him when his schedule permitted. However, she, like so many other Americans, was shocked and saddened by the news of his assassination on April 14, 1865.

Securing Government Aid and Money

With Lincoln gone, Barton began pressing for aid from other high-ranking government officials, including the new president, Andrew Johnson. At one point, she persuaded him to put the Government Printing Office at her disposal. That office proceeded to publish twenty thousand copies of the rolls of missing men she and her helpers had been compiling. Also, Henry Wilson gave her money from his own pockets to defray part of the huge expense of mailing these lists.

With these resources, Barton's crew sent the lists to every post office in the North. They also circulated copies to every army camp and town hall. In addition, Barton composed an open letter to the American people. "You, too, must cooperate," it said,

> or the work cannot be done. You will excuse me for speaking very frankly on this point, for the work is yours. . . . it is for you to say whether it is worth doing. If it costs the United States four thousand dollars to kill an enemy in battle, is it worth five dollars or ten dollars to discover the fate of a citizen who has been reported missing? If then you approve of my work, I ask you to give your . . . support.[3]

This sign for Barton's missing soldiers office was discovered in 2002 in the long-neglected attic of a commercial building in Washington, D.C., where she once lived.

As a result of all this public exposure, Barton's search for missing soldiers became known to people all across the country. And the volume of letters asking for help increased greatly. Soon the office was receiving more than 150 letters each day. Luckily, the office acquired official status as a minor government agency. In 1866, thanks to the efforts of Wilson and some other sympathetic senators, the U.S. Senate provided some funding.

The Senate also voted to pay Barton fifteen thousand dollars to reimburse her for her earlier outlay of personal funds. She continued to funnel her own money into the cause. Between 1866 and 1868, she delivered more than three hundred lectures. Crowds flocked to hear her stirring accounts of her war experiences. And she donated most of the money she earned for these speeches to the missing soldiers office.

Prison of Death

Barton's publication of lists of missing men also involved her in an important issue she had not anticipated. When these lists went public, her work became known to a former Union soldier named Dorence Atwater. He had been a prisoner at Andersonville. Located at Camp Sumter, in west-central Georgia, Andersonville was the largest of the Confederate military prisons. Some forty-five thousand prisoners were kept there at one time or another. Overcrowding, too little food and clean water, disease, and lack of proper medical treatment took an awful toll. Nearly thirteen thousand prisoners died in the prison.

Andersonville's Deplorable Conditions

Reaching the dreaded Andersonville Prison in July 1865, Barton surveyed the twenty-six-and-a-half-acre enclosure. Her guide, Dorence Atwater, told her that it had originally been designed for ten thousand prisoners. Yet at times it had held as many as forty-five thousand. The guards had provided the inmates no shelter from the weather. Many men had improvised little tents from coats or blankets. Others had dug little burrows in the slope of a hill that lay within the enclosure wall. They held back the dirt with sticks or boards.

Barton also learned that the only water available to the prisoners came from a nearby stream. Unfortunately, the water was almost constantly polluted. The latrines overflowed into it, and the camp's cookhouse dumped its refuse into it. In desperation, some men had used spoons and sticks to dig wells in hopes of finding fresh water. But what little water they found had a high concentration of sulfur. In addition, the prisoners had been overrun by maggots and other vermin. In such deplorable conditions, Barton, concluded, it was no wonder that so many prisoners had died.

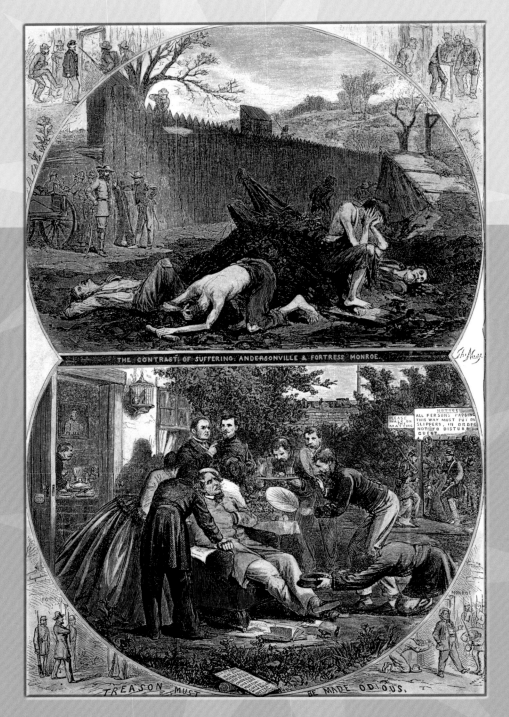

An 1866 cartoon by Thomas Nast contrasted the suffering endured by Federal prisoners of war with the luxurious treatment given to Confederate President Jefferson Davis, then a prisoner at Fort Monroe, Virginia.

The commander of the prison had assigned Atwater the task of keeping track of these deceased men. When one died, he wrote down his name, state, military unit, cause of death, and the date. But he worried that the information he was giving the guards would be lost or destroyed at war's end. So he kept a secret duplicate list. And now he offered this list to Clara Barton. She was thrilled because she could compare the names on the list with those on her own lists of missing men. Almost thirteen thousand missing soldiers would be accounted for this way.

Barton also determined to go to Andersonville and create a proper cemetery for the dead prisoners there.

Barton also determined to go to Andersonville and create a proper cemetery for the dead prisoners there. She met with Secretary of War Edwin Stanton and he strongly endorsed the idea. He ordered the formation of an expedition headed by Captain James M. Moore. Accompanied by Barton and Atwater, the unit headed south on July 8, 1865, and reached Andersonville on July 26. The next day, Barton and the others began the task of making a white headstone for each of 12,913 dead prisoners. And on August 17, she had the honor of raising the American flag over the newly created cemetery.

Memories of Death and Life

Following the trip to Georgia, Clara Barton returned to Annapolis and resumed her work in the missing-soldiers office. The tireless efforts of that little agency finally ended late in 1868. In a final report to Congress, she listed its considerable accomplishments. She and her assistants had received and studied 63,182 inquiries. They had written 41,855 letters, mailed 58,693 information sheets, distributed 99,057 lists of missing men, and identified more than 22,000 missing soldiers. Barton estimated that the 40,000 or so men still unaccounted for at that time were dead.[4] Regrettably, she stated, their graves, if any, would not likely be found.

Having filed this report, Barton officially closed the office in Annapolis. For her it marked the end of some seven years of dedicated and grueling war-related service to her country. Yet in a way, her connections to that awful conflict had not been severed. She still gave lectures recounting her harrowing experiences on bloody battlefields.

These speeches were often difficult for Barton to deliver. Indeed, they brought back memories of horrible carnage and promising lives snuffed out. From time to time, someone came forward to remind her of the lives she had saved.

One day, following a lecture in a YMCA, a man, accompanied by a little girl, approached her. He told Barton that she had saved his life at Second Bull Run. Later, in a battle fought near Fredericksburg, she had saved him again. "My hands and feet were frozen," he recalled. "You had the men scrape the snow off the ground and gave [me] warm drink and kept hot bricks about [me] all night." Incredibly, the man continued,

Washington, D. C., , 186

Gentlemen and Ladies —

I come before you to-night both willingly and cheerfully — more than willing to render my account for the unmeasured kindness received of the American people. and the great confidence reposed in me by the officers and men of the army. during the trials of the past few years.

If I have been allowed to perform a work, among the armies of my country, withheld from many others: and have thereby learned facts unknown to them. it is my duty to state them when required.

This handwritten copy of one of Barton's speeches was one she gave while working for the missing soldiers office.

their paths had crossed again on a third battlefield, where she had alleviated his hunger and thirst. "Your care saved my life," he told her warmly.

"And is this your little girl?" Barton asked.

"Yes," he answered proudly. "She is almost three years old. And we call her Clara Barton."[5]

Creation of the American Red Cross

In 1869, Clara Barton was forty-seven. But she felt much older. Her many years of tireless efforts on the battlefield, in the missing soldiers office, and on the lecture circuit had exhausted her. And she now endured frequent headaches, earaches, and bouts of heavy coughing. Her doctors ordered her to take a long rest and suggested recuperating in Europe.

With her sister, Sally Vassal, Barton first spent some time in Scotland, which both women found pleasant and restful. Sally then returned to the United States. But Clara Barton went on to Geneva, Switzerland. There, she stayed at the home of Jules Golay, a Swiss citizen who had aided her during the Civil War.

A Fateful Meeting

One day while she was resting in Golay's house, which overlooked a lovely lake, some visitors came to see Barton. This fateful meeting ended up opening a major new chapter in her life. Golay had often bragged about Barton's war heroics to some prominent European friends. Among them was Dr. Louis Appia.

With a colleague, Henri Dunant, Appia ran a humanitarian organization called the International Convention of Geneva, or Geneva Convention for short. It was also more commonly referred to as the International Committee of the Red Cross. This name was inspired by the group's symbol—a red cross emblazoned on a white background. The Geneva Convention/Red Cross provided ambulances and battlefield hospitals during wartime. It also ensured that its volunteers would be treated as neutrals. In other words, they would be respected and protected by both sides in a war.

In the course of Barton's meeting with Appia, he asked her why the Americans had so far refused to join the Geneva Convention. At its inception in 1864, he told her, eleven countries had signed the treaty.

And by 1869, that number had increased to thirty-two. She replied that she had never heard of the organization. Moreover, she said, she was "sure the American people did not know anything about it." Nor did she understand why the U.S. government had "carelessly stumbled over this jewel and trodden it underfeet to the astonishment of all the world."[1]

Henri Dunant

The Relief Effort at Strasbourg

Barton soon had a chance to see this "jewel" of an organization in action. On July 18, 1870, while she was still in Switzerland, France declared war on Prussia (a part of what is now Germany). This initiated the so-called Franco-Prussian War, which lasted about a year. Though she had not yet fully regained her health, Barton could not suppress her urge to help soldiers in need. So she volunteered to work for the International Red Cross.

Appia happily welcomed Barton and took her to the group's warehouse in Basel, Switzerland. In this large storage facility, she saw enormous amounts of medical supplies and food. These supplies had been donated by the Geneva Convention member countries for use by any soldiers that needed them. It was "a larger supply [of relief materials] than I had ever seen at any one time," she later wrote. She was also amazed to see hundreds of nurses and aid workers "awaiting their appointment, each with this badge [the red cross] upon the arm or breast."[2]

Displaying her usual courage and audacity, Barton joined up with a young Red Cross worker named Antoinette Margot. The two made their way through the French countryside in hopes of reaching one of the conflict's main battlefronts. Along the way, they had a number of scary run-ins with German soldiers. But in each case, the women managed to escape.

Finally, Barton and Margot reached the French town of Strasbourg, which had been badly damaged in the fighting. They quickly set up makeshift hospitals and soup kitchens. Barton also pioneered a policy that would later become a hallmark of Red Cross chapters across the world. She organized groups of local citizens to begin rebuilding the ruined houses, stores, and churches. These workers were paid for their efforts partly by Red Cross contributions and partly by their local government.

The people of Strasbourg looked on Barton, as Dr. James Dunn had, as an angel who had come to their rescue. On her birthday, on Christmas Day in 1871, they thanked her with a special gift. That morning there was a knock on her door. Opening it, she beheld an enormous, elaborately decorated Christmas tree, surrounded by a huge crowd of well-wishers.

The Kernel of a Noble Idea

As usual, Clara Barton proved more passionate about *giving* gifts than receiving them. Increasingly, she wanted to give her own countrymen the gift of the Red Cross. She later remembered how the kernel of this noble idea took shape:

> [I witnessed] order, plenty, cleanliness, and comfort wherever that little [Red Cross] flag made its way —a whole continent marshaled under the banner of the Red Cross—as I saw all this, and joined and worked in it, you will not wonder that I said to myself, "If I live to return to my country, I will try to make my people understand the Red Cross and that treaty [Geneva Convention]."[3]

In spite of this sincere goal, Barton was not able to fulfill it immediately. When she returned to the United States in October 1873, she was both exhausted and ill. Her headaches had returned with a vengeance. And she suffered from periods of near blindness and an inability to walk, or even to stand. During her recovery, she spent some time in her hometown in Massachusetts. She also recuperated at a clinic in Dansville, a small town in northwestern New York State. There, one of the young Swiss women she had worked with in Europe acted as her nurse and faithful companion.

"I will try to make my people understand the Red Cross."

Barton longed to organize an American unit of the Red Cross.

Over time, Barton felt progressively stronger. She longed to organize an American unit of the Red Cross. The immediate spark for this effort came one day in 1877. She read in the newspaper that a war was brewing between Russia and Turkey. In a letter to Dr. Appia, she laid out some of her ideas. One was that the American Red Cross could collect money and supplies from Americans and ship them to needy folks in Europe.

Encouraging Letters from Europe

Appia promptly wrote back, encouraging Barton to proceed with her plans for establishing an American version of the Red Cross. She also received a letter from Gustave Moynier, then director of the International Red Cross. He named her the official American representative of the International Red Cross. In addition, he enclosed a letter addressed to the sitting U.S. president, Rutherford B. Hayes. It requested that the U.S. government sign the Geneva Convention. It also urged Hayes and his officials to work with Barton to establish an American Red Cross unit. "Mr. President," Moynier's letter began,

> The International Committee of the Red Cross desires most earnestly that the United States should be associated with them in their work . . . [which involves] those humanitarian principles

now admitted by all civilized people. . . . We only wait [the] good news . . . [of] the founding of an American Society of the Red Cross. We have already an able and devoted assistant in Miss Clara Barton, to whom we confide the care of handing to you this present request.[4]

The letters from Moynier jolted Barton into action. She left her sickbed and began taking stock of her contacts in high places in Washington. It was clear that she would need all the political allies she could find to achieve the new mission. Some of her old Washington friends, including Henry Wilson, were now deceased. But she found other supporters in the U.S. Congress.

When Barton approached President Hayes, however, she was in for a disappointment. He referred her to the U.S. attorney general, who then sent her to other, lower-ranking officials. Finally, she met with the assistant secretary of state, Frederick W. Seward. He told her that there was virtually no chance of the United States signing the Geneva Convention. Nor would the country become a member of the International Red Cross. Such moves might allow Europeans to meddle in American affairs, he said. Anyway, Seward added, the United States would never be fighting a war in Europe. So what need was there of belonging to a European relief organization?

An Enormous Triumph

Barton was sorely disappointed by the negative reaction she had received from government officials. But she was

A Home for War's Disabled

The symbol of the Red Cross has become famous and recognized across the world. In one of her many lectures about the organization, Clara Barton said the following about the symbol and what it means for soldiers in wartime:

The Red Cross flag

A Greek red cross on a field of white should tell any soldier of any country within the treaty [Geneva Convention] that the wearer [is] his friend and [can] be trusted. . . . From every military hospital in every one of these nations, floats the same [Red Cross] flag; and every active soldier in all their armies knows that he can neither capture nor harm the shelter beneath it . . . and every disabled man knows it is his rescue and his home.[5]

determined to keep trying. She continued to promote the idea of an American Red Cross, this time trying a new approach. So far, she had mainly emphasized the value of such an organization during wartime. Now she pointed out that even if the country never got into a foreign war, the Red Cross would still be useful. In particular, it could offer aid to victims of natural disasters in the United States. "Seldom a year passes," she wrote in a pamphlet:

> *that the nation from sea to sea is not [stricken by] some sudden, unforeseen disaster . . . Plagues, cholera, fires, flood, famine,—all bear upon us with terrible force. . . . What have we in readiness to meet these emergencies save for the good heart of our people?*[6]

Partly thanks to this new emphasis on disaster aid, Barton began to stir up interest in Washington's halls of power. In 1880, James A. Garfield was elected president. He and several influential senators seemed ready to support her goals. That inspired Barton to go ahead and establish an unofficial American Red Cross

The first American Red Cross building was in Dansville, New York.

The Red Cross Always Ready

During her long association with the American Red Cross, Clara Barton repeatedly emphasized the concept of readiness. In the preface of her own history of the organization, first published in 1898, she wrote:

Through all the past years, during which the Red Cross has sought recognition, protection and cooperation, it was but for one purpose—to be ready. . . . Before us now lie the problems of the future, and the question is: How shall we meet them? As friends of humanity, while there is still a possibility of war or calamity, it behooves us to prepare. . . . Certainly in no other country have the people so often risen from a state of unreadiness and accomplished such wonderful results—at such a great sacrifice. . . . it is the purpose of the Red Cross . . . to continue its work of preparation, until in its councils and in its ranks the whole country shall be represented, standing together, ready for any great emergency, inspired by the love of humanity and the worldwide motto of the Red Cross: "In time of peace and prosperity, prepare for war and calamity."[7]

NO.

THE AMERICAN NATIONAL RED CROSS

EMERGENCY CASE

First Aid to the Injured

CONTENTS.

Emergency Chart Indexed for Instantaneous Reference, containing brief, simple Instructions for rendering emergency treatment; covering the whole range of Accidents liable to occur in Households, Factories, Railroads, Schools, and all places of public resort; and designed as a means of averting fatal results pending the arrival of the Doctor.

A full supply of Surgical Dressings &c., for emergency treatment specially selected by the Surgical and Medical Staff of the New York Red Cross Hospital, and prepared under the supervision of the Red Cross Sisters.

TO CONSULT EMERGENCY CHART UNFASTEN HOOK SECURING OUTSIDE COVER.

WHEN NECESSARY TO USE CONTENTS LIFT CASE FROM HOOK AND SLIDE COVER TO THE LEFT.

First Aid Department

No. 31 East Seventeenth Street, NEW YORK.

One of the original American Red Cross first aid kits is displayed at the Clara Barton birthplace and museum in North Oxford, Massachusetts.

organization on May 11, 1881. She was hopeful that official government approval would come in the near future.

Soon afterward, however, in September of that year, Garfield was assassinated. For a few weeks, it looked as though Barton's cause was lost. Or at least she might have to start from scratch in promoting the Geneva Convention and Red Cross. But then, quite unexpectedly, nature, or fate, or both intervened. In the late summer and early fall of 1881, enormous forest fires raged through parts of Michigan. More than five thousand people became homeless. Barton's newly formed Red Cross unit immediately sprang into action, shipping tons of food, clothes, and other supplies to Michigan. In all, the group raised more than eighty thousand dollars to help the homeless.

To many Americans, Barton now seemed like a prophet. Her predictions about the value of the Red Cross, even in peacetime, had come true. The political winds were now at her back. And on March 16, 1882, the U.S. Congress, with the support of President Chester A. Arthur, ratified the Geneva Convention. The United States now became a member of the International Committee of the Red Cross. As one of Barton's modern biographers writes, it was "an enormous triumph" for her. "The American Red Cross stands, [more than] one hundred years later, a monument to Clara Barton's foresight, courage, and perseverance."[8]

Barton's Red Cross in Action

The disastrous fires that swept through Michigan in 1881 brought the Red Cross to the attention of the American people. Thereafter, the organization became a permanent and respected fixture of the American scene. Clara Barton served as president of the Red Cross from its inception until 1904. Almost every year during this period, some natural disaster or human conflict created large numbers of needy people. And almost without exception, Barton and her colleagues rose to each new challenge. Red Cross workers raised money to purchase relief supplies and fed the hungry. Sometimes they even risked their own lives to save disaster victims from imminent death.

The Ohio Valley Floods

The lifesaving role that Barton's organization played became national news again in 1884. That year the Ohio and Mississippi rivers overflowed their banks. Large sections of the American Midwest suffered severe flooding. As Barton herself described it:

> *For hundreds of miles, the great [Ohio] river was out of its bed and raging madly over the country . . . [It swept away] not only the homes but often the people, [and] the animals . . . leaving them clinging in famishing despair to some trembling roof or swaying treetop.* [1]

Many of these "trembling roofs" were in the city of Cincinnati, Ohio, which was almost completely underwater. Numerous victims had to be rescued by boat. "The surging river had climbed up the bluffs like a devouring monster and possessed the town," Barton later recalled. Victims, she said, reached out "from third-story windows of stately blocks and warehouses of that beautiful city. Sometimes the water soaked away the foundations [of a building] and the structure fell with a crash."[2]

Chartering a small ship, the *Josh V. Throop*, Barton filled it with relief materials. She then navigated the

Six children who initiated the first American Red Cross youth activity in Waterford, Pa., raised fifty dollars, which they gave to Clara Barton to help victims of the 1884 floods in the Ohio Valley.

swollen rivers, distributing food, blankets, and medical supplies to thousands of homeless people. Barton and her followers also helped many of these people rebuild their damaged homes. In all, the *Throop*'s errand of mercy carried it more than eight thousand miles in only four months.

Off to Geneva

Exhausted by her nonstop efforts in the Ohio Valley, in the fall of 1884 Barton planned to take some time off and rest. But this was not to be. Arriving home, she found urgent pleas for her to go to Geneva, Switzerland. The annual conference of the International Red Cross was scheduled for late September. Both the International Committee and the U.S. government wanted Barton to represent the United States.

This was a great honor in and of itself. Making it more unusual was the fact that Barton was the only female delegate at the conference. More remarkable still was what she achieved there. She suggested amending the International Committee's charter to state that war victims were not the only people the Red Cross would aid. Red Cross chapters around the globe should also help victims of natural disasters, she said. As proof of the importance of such aid, she pointed out the American unit's recent relief efforts in Michigan and Ohio.

Some of the delegates disagreed with Barton. They felt that the Red Cross should limit its activities to wartime situations. But a majority agreed with her. The International Committee adopted her proposal, calling it the "American Amendment." Thus, in addition to creating the American Red Cross, Barton helped to shape the future of the International Red Cross.

A Series of Catastrophes

Barton's emphasis on aiding disaster victims proved prophetic in the years that followed. A series of natural catastrophes struck both inside and outside the United States between 1885 and 1892. She committed the growing resources of the American Red Cross to helping the victims of these disasters.

In 1885 and 1886, for example, Barton's organization came to the aid of drought victims in Texas. "For fifteen months no rain had fallen," she later wrote. "The condition of the people was pitiable and called aloud . . . for relief."[3] Because of the lack of rain, the local wheat crop had failed, and thousands of people were starving. Barton and her followers quickly supplied more than one hundred thousand dollars worth of food, an enormous amount at the time, thereby alleviating the suffering.

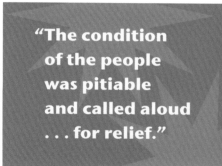

"The condition of the people was pitiable and called aloud . . . for relief."

After that, disaster after disaster kept Barton and her organization almost constantly busy. In 1888, they assisted victims of yellow fever in an outbreak of that dreaded disease in Florida. The following spring, news came of an enormous flood in Johnstown, Pennsylvania.

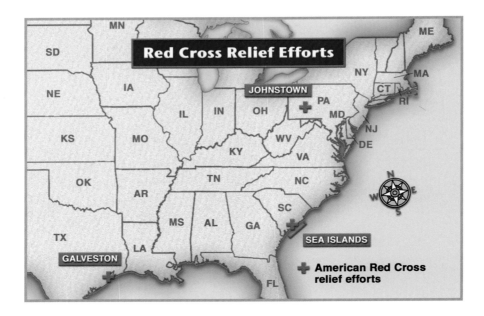

Made worse by the collapse of a dam, the flooding killed more than two thousand people. Thousands more were homeless. For five months Barton, then sixty-eight years old, lived in a tent in crude conditions, coordinating disaster aid day and night. The American Red Cross also sent thousands of dollars worth of food to Russia when a terrible famine swept that country from 1891 to 1892.

The Sea Islands Disaster

Perhaps the most heroic and memorable achievements of the American Red Cross in this period occurred in 1893. In August of that year, a monstrous hurricane struck South Carolina. Hit hardest were the Sea Islands, off the state's southern coast. At least five thousand people died in a single night, and more than thirty thousand others became homeless and destitute. "The gaunt figure of famine," Barton said, "silently drew near and stared them in the face."[4]

Barton was appalled not only by the loss of life, but also by the government's failure to react to the disaster. The problem was that most of the victims were poor African Americans. Because of racial prejudice, white officials, both in South Carolina and Washington, did almost nothing. Even the head of a noted charitable organization was reluctant to help. He told Barton that giving blacks free food would make them "lazy and worthless and probably uncontrollable."[5]

Women cut potatoes for planting as part of the Sea Island Red Cross relief effort.

Barton was shocked and saddened by these ignorant, insensitive, and inhumane opinions. She argued that it would be a national disgrace to ignore the plight of the Sea Islands residents and quickly initiated relief efforts. Red Cross nurses tended to injured people. Meanwhile, wagons brought loads of lumber to rebuild houses that had been damaged in the hurricane. Barton's workers also collected old clothes from across South Carolina and beyond. With the help of the Sea Islands residents themselves, the Red Cross washed and distributed the garments to those in need.

The most impressive achievement of the relief effort was the manner in which Barton and her workers fed the hungry. At the time, the Red Cross's funds were almost gone. There was not enough money to pay for shipping in immense quantities of food from the outside. So, in a creative and cost-effective move, the Red Cross brought seeds. Barton's workers helped the locals plant and tend vegetable gardens. One leading Red Cross official later recalled:

> *Miss Barton sent to the Ohio valley for two carloads of seed corn. This was distributed over the entire storm-swept section, and many of these people at harvest time said . . . their crop was double what it had ever been before.*[6]

In this way, Barton and her followers saved thirty thousand afflicted Sea Islanders from mass starvation. A number of the grateful residents expressed their thanks by volunteering their services to the Red Cross during later disasters.

Victims of Brutal Conflicts

Natural disasters were not the only emergencies that Clara Barton and her followers confronted during the Red Cross's early years. Wars were still an unfortunate and persistent reality of the international scene. And Barton frequently committed her organization's

Vast Amounts of Money

One reason that Barton's American Red Cross was able to render so much aid to war and disaster victims was that the organization raised vast amounts of money. All of it came from private donations. In fact, during Barton's watch, the Red Cross received no funds from the U.S. government.

In her 1898 history of the Red Cross, Barton provided estimates of the amounts spent during various emergencies. Helping the victims of the 1881 Michigan fires cost about $80,000, for example. The 1884 Ohio River floods absorbed $175,000 of Red Cross money. And Barton spent more than $250,000 to alleviate the suffering caused by the 1889 Johnstown Floods.[7] To put these figures in perspective, multiply each by 27. That adjusts for inflation over the years and reveals how much these monies are worth more than a century later.

The Coming of World Peace?

During Clara Barton's time as president of the American Red Cross, that organization saved tens of thousands of lives. And it did so without asking for anything in return. Indeed, Barton's workers received no salaries or other payments for their efforts. At the time, a number of journalists and other observers drew public attention to this unselfishness. Some even predicted that the emergence of the Red Cross somehow foreshadowed the coming of permanent world peace. Newspaper editorials also expressed this overly optimistic view, including one from a midwestern paper, the *Inter-Ocean*, in 1884:

> *In its work among suffering humanity . . . the Red Cross seeks to carry to people's hearts that message which speaks of a universal brotherhood. It is all the time and everywhere sowing the seed of brotherly kindness and goodwill, which is destined in time to yield the fruits of world-wide peace. . . . arsenals and iron-clad navies will give way to the spirit of equity. War will cease as a relic of barbarism, and peace will shed its benedictions over all nations.*[8]

resources to helping the innocent victims of brutal conflicts.

Not long after the Sea Islands hurricane, for instance, she responded to a call for aid from Turkey. That nation had recently been wracked by a religious war. Many of the survivors were suffering from disease and lack of food. Barton spent ten months in Turkey passing out essential supplies, an effort that saved thousands of lives.

Another of Barton's war-related relief efforts began to take shape in 1897 in Cuba. That large island, lying south of Florida, was then controlled by Spain. Spanish officials in Cuba had been trying to defeat bands of revolutionaries who wanted independence from Spain. Many of the rebel sympathizers were herded into camps. Large numbers of those confined were women and children, and many nations pressured Spain to provide aid to these victims. As a result, Barton and her helpers were allowed to dispense food and other supplies in the Cuban camps.

The Spanish-American War

Barton and the Red Cross were still in Cuba when the Spanish-American War erupted early in 1898. In fact, she was working in her makeshift headquarters in Havana on the fateful evening of February 15. "Suddenly the table shook from under our hands," she later remembered:

> *The great glass door opening onto the veranda, facing the sea, flew open; everything in the room*

Clara Barton and other members of the American Red Cross walk down a street in Cuba during the Spanish-American War.

was in motion or out of place. [We heard] the deafening roar of such a burst of thunder as perhaps one never heard before. . . . the air was filled with a blaze of light, and this in turn filled with black specks like huge [ghosts] flying in all directions.[9]

Barton and her coworkers had just witnessed history in the making. Not far away, in Havana's harbor, the U.S. Navy battleship *Maine* had blown apart in a gigantic explosion. More than 260 American sailors were killed. Afterward, Barton and her colleagues treated many of the wounded.

No one ever figured out who destroyed the *Maine*. But the U.S. government ultimately blamed Spain. On April 25, 1898, the United States declared war on Spain. As part of the war effort, President William McKinley authorized Clara Barton to charter a relief ship. That vessel, the *State of Texas*, soon carried more than fourteen hundred tons of supplies into the heart of the conflict.

At age seventy-six, Barton displayed the energy, determination, and raw courage of a person half her age. Ignoring danger, she set up several makeshift hospitals near active battlefronts. These medical facilities treated both American troops and Spanish soldiers that had been captured. The latter were at first terrified. Their generals had told them that if they were captured,

This 1899 calendar shows an American Red Cross nurse comforting a much decorated soldier with a letter from home just after the Spanish-American War. Ironically, more casualties resulted from disease and tainted beef than from battle.

the Americans would slaughter them. The Spanish prisoners were pleasantly surprised, therefore, when they received excellent treatment. This happened largely because American commanders followed the humanitarian principles advocated by the Geneva Convention and the Red Cross.

An Avalanche of Praise

Barton was pleased when hostilities between Spain and the United States halted on August 12, 1898. Spain soon sued for peace, and the two countries signed a peace treaty in December. That same month, in a speech to the U.S. Congress, President William McKinley heartily thanked Barton and her Red Cross workers. He was not the only one who called attention to the important role she had played in the American victory. In the words of one leading official, she had "performed her [difficult] duties during the entire war with a devotion and earnestness that merit universal recognition at home and abroad."[10]

Indeed, Barton had by then become one of the most famous and beloved women in the world. Yet she remained as humble and selfless as ever. Her response to the avalanche of praise heaped on her was: "Our only regret is that, during the late war, we were not able to render greater service."[11]

9

Final Battles and a Living Legacy

In some ways, the Spanish-American War proved to be a major turning point in Clara Barton's life. When she returned to the United States from Cuba late in 1898, she found herself facing some unexpected difficulties. Barton was used to dealing with the trials of wars and natural catastrophes. But she was not prepared for challenges to her leadership within her own organization. A number of her Red Cross colleagues now began to question her methods. Some even felt that she was not fit to continue as leader of the group.

Most of the initial complaints against her concerned the way she had handled the organization's supplies and funds. While in Cuba, for example, she had given some relief supplies to American soldiers. Her critics pointed out that these materials had been intended for needy Cubans. Supplies set aside for one group should not be given to another, the critics said. Barton saw these arguments as misguided. In her view, wars and disasters create needy people of all kinds. Red Cross workers should have the ability to decide who is most in need at any given place and time.

Some of Barton's critics within the Red Cross also claimed that she had used the group's funds to pay for her personal luxuries. Those closest to her knew that this charge was baseless. In truth, she had a frugal lifestyle and denied herself luxuries. Another charge was that Barton had not kept accurate, detailed records of the Red Cross monies she had spent over the years. One critic admitted that she was honest and well-meaning. But, he added, "We do think that there has been a great deal of carelessness."[1]

Barton and her supporters conceded that some minor mistakes had undoubtedly been made. But no funds had been intentionally misused. In fact, a later investigation cleared Barton of any financial or other wrongdoing. The investigators said that she had kept the best records humanly possible in the chaotic conditions in which she worked.

Clara Barton in 1904

Duty Calls Once Again

During the same period in which criticisms of Barton's leadership emerged, another major disaster struck the United States. On September 8, 1900, an enormous hurricane hammered Galveston, Texas. About four thousand homes and other structures were destroyed. And at least six thousand people died. (Some estimates put the death toll above ten thousand.)

Once more, Barton felt it was her duty to aid those in need. She and eight assistants arrived in Galveston a few days after the storm.

> **"It was one of those monstrosities of nature which defied exaggeration."**

Though she had seen much devastation in her life, the wreckage she viewed there left her shaken and awestruck. "It was one of those monstrosities of nature which defied exaggeration," she later wrote.

> *The churches, the great business houses, the elegant residences of the cultured and opulent [rich], the modest little homes of laborers of a city of nearly forty thousand people . . . [all] lay in splinters and debris piled twenty feet above the surface, and the crushed bodies, dead and dying, of nearly ten thousand of its citizens lay under them.*[2]

After surveying the damage, the seventy-eight-year-old Barton got to work. She issued emergency appeals to every corner of the country. And because of her reputation as a humanitarian, tens of thousands of people responded. "She served as a magnet," one modern observer points out. "People sent money and goods . . . to Clara Barton because they trusted her and they knew her work."[3] For instance, some Pennsylvania steelworkers whom she had helped during the Johnstown flood sent cash. Meanwhile, people in other states sent clothing, shoes, blankets, food, medical supplies, and other materials. In all, more than one hundred twenty thousand dollars in money and supplies poured into the stricken city through the Red Cross.

How Should the Red Cross Be Run?

When Clara Barton left Galveston in November 1900, she did not realize that she had reached another turning point in her life. The Galveston disaster was to be the last national emergency she would deal with in person. Her final few years at the Red Cross would be dominated instead by arguments over agency policy and methods.

To her dismay, Barton found that her critics in the organization wanted to institute major changes. First, they addressed the issue of leadership. It was not good, they said, for the Red Cross to have a single leader with so much authority. They thought that it would be fairer and more efficient to have several leaders in the form of a board of directors.

Also, some of the critics questioned one of the core principles of the Red Cross—volunteerism. No one, including Barton, received any payment for their charitable work. In fact, for years she had contributed money from her own bank account to run the Red Cross. In contrast, a number of the group's higher officials now wanted to receive salaries. Members of their staffs also wanted to be paid. Barton did not agree with these and other proposed changes. She felt that they went against the original high ideals of the Red Cross.

Active in Retirement

Barton's opposition to change was one reason that she resigned her position as president of the Red Cross in May 1904. The other was her age. At eighty-two, she lacked the enormous reserves of energy she had once possessed.

Nevertheless, Barton remained active in retirement. In 1905, she established the National Association of First Aid. This organization's mission was to train volunteers in American towns to bandage wounds and provide immediate care. The group was not meant to be a rival or competitor of the Red Cross. Rather, the goal was to teach ordinary citizens to deal with minor first aid emergencies that were too small-scale for the Red Cross to bother with. Barton also continued to give lectures and help worthy causes. One of these was the growing movement in support of women's suffrage— allowing women to vote.

Barton was no less active in her private life. In her home in Glen Echo, Maryland, she rose early each morning to milk a cow she kept on the property. She also owned and rode a horse named Baba and churned her own butter. Her days were devoted to reading and answering the many letters she received from well-wishers. Barton also received numerous offers from writers who wanted to tell her life story. She finally gave permission to two men to write authorized biographies. One was a friend and Protestant minister, Percy Epler. The other was her cousin William E. Barton.

"She Will Be With Us Always"

As time went on, however, the once tireless Barton grew steadily weaker and less able to fend off illness. In January 1912, she contracted pneumonia and she never fully recovered. For the next few months, she remained in bed at the Glen Echo house. Moreover, due to heavy medication she slept much of the time. On April 10, she awoke and told her close friend, Dr. Julian Hubble, about a dream she had just had. In the dream she had found herself back on a Civil War battlefield, tending to wounded soldiers. Two days later, on April 12, 1912, she briefly awoke again. "Let me go, let me go," she murmured.[4] A few seconds later, she passed away at age ninety.

"Let me go, let me go."

Barton's funeral took place a few days later in her hometown of North Oxford, Massachusetts. Reverend Epler led the services, which were attended by hundreds of people. Among them were many former soldiers who had come to pay their respects to the "angel of the battlefield." Her surviving relatives buried her less than a mile from the old family house.

By the time the United States entered World War I in 1917, the American Red Cross was a well-established institution.

Barton's Antietam Memorial

One of the many memorials honoring Clara Barton's achievements and memory rests on the battlefield of Antietam. There, at the height of the American Civil War, she risked her life to save hundreds of wounded soldiers. It was also during the bloody, chaotic days that she spent there that she received the nickname "angel of the battlefield." In 1890, the U.S. government established the Antietam National Battlefield. Among the many stone markers raised there to honor the heroes of the battle is one bearing these words:

CLARA BARTON. During the battle of Antietam, September 17, 1862, Clara Barton brought supplies and nursing aid to the wounded on this battlefield. This act of love and mercy led to the birth of the present AMERICAN NATIONAL RED CROSS.[5]

In the years that followed, Barton received many other tributes from those who had known her and many who had not. Schools, parks, and roads across the country were named for her. And in 1942, during World War II, the U.S. Navy named a supply ship after her—the U.S.S. *Clara Barton*. Later still, in 1975, the U.S. government made her Glen Echo house a national historic site. It was the first national historic site dedicated to a woman.

On September 2, 2005, a Red Cross volunteer comforts a victim of Hurricane Katrina in the Houston Astrodome. Approximately eighteen thousand Hurricane Katrina survivors were sheltered in the Red Cross facility at the Astrodome and Reliant Center.

However, Clara Barton's greatest and most enduring memorial is the organization she founded in 1881. Today, the American Red Cross remains one of the world's leading humanitarian organizations. It directly employs more than thirty thousand people. And more than a million people of all walks of life volunteer to help Red Cross workers each year. These combined forces annually deliver aid in thousands of emergencies, big and small. They also provide more than 40 percent of the country's donated blood.

In a very real way, therefore, the people the Red Cross helps today become part of Clara Barton's ongoing living legacy. Each year the organization helps people struck by all sorts of natural and manmade disasters. Some well-known examples include the 9/11 attacks in New York City and Washington, D.C., in 2001 and Hurricane Katrina, which battered Louisiana and Mississippi in 2005. The thanks the victims of such disasters give to modern Red Cross workers often mimic those of the people Barton aided in her lifetime. In that regard, the memory of her achievements is eternally illuminated by the words of some of the survivors of the Johnstown flood. "We cannot thank Miss Barton in words," they said:

> *Hunt the dictionaries of all languages . . . and you will not find the signs to express our appreciation. . . . She is with us, she will be with us always [in the form of] the spirit of her work even after she has passed away.*[6]

CHRONOLOGY

1821—Clara Barton is born on Christmas Day in North Oxford, Massachusetts.

1832–1834—Nurses her seriously injured brother David back to health.

1840—Begins teaching in a small schoolhouse in the neighboring community of Charlton.

1850—Enrolls at the Clinton Liberal Institute, a teachers' preparatory school in Clinton, New York.

1854—Takes a job at the U.S. Patent Office in Washington, D.C.

1861—The American Civil War begins. Barton sees a need for volunteers to aid wounded troops.

1862—Risking her own life, she tends to wounded soldiers at the battles of Antietam, Cedar Mountain, and Second Bull Run.

1864—Is appointed superintendent of nurses for a division of Union soldiers. The International Red Cross is established in Europe.

1865—The Civil War ends. Barton begins a nationwide search for missing soldiers.

1869—Badly needing a rest, she travels to Europe and stays at a friend's house in Switzerland.

1870—The Franco-Prussian war erupts, and Barton volunteers to help the International Red Cross.

1877—Now back in the United States, she begins to promote the idea of an American chapter of the Red Cross.

1881—Establishes the American Red Cross. The new organization faces its first major test when huge fires ravage parts of Michigan.

1884—The Red Cross renders aid to victims of terrible floods in the Ohio Valley.

1889—Barton and her followers relieve the suffering of thousands of people during the Johnstown flood in Pennsylvania.

1893—In a heroic effort, Barton and the Red Cross save thirty thousand people in South Carolina from starvation following the devastating Sea Islands hurricane.

1898—Barton distributes supplies and medical care in Cuba during the Spanish-American War.

1904—At age eighty-two, Barton resigns her position as president of the American Red Cross.

1912—Clara Barton, age ninety, dies from complications of pneumonia at her home in Glen Echo, Maryland.

CHAPTER NOTES

CHAPTER 1
An Angel on the Battlefield

1. Cornelius Welles, "Dear Brethren," newspaper clipping dated September 22, 1862, in *Clara Barton Papers*, Library of Congress, Washington, D.C.
2. Paddy Griffith, *Battle Tactics of the Civil War* (New Haven: Yale University Press, 2001), p. 19.
3. Quoted from a lecture given by Clara Barton on February 14, 1863, in *Clara Barton Papers*, Library of Congress, Washington, D.C.
4. Quoted in Clara Barton, "Work and Incidents," in *Clara Barton Papers*, Library of Congress, Washington, D.C.
5. Ibid.
6. James Dunn, "The Angel of the Battlefield," undated newspaper clipping, in *Clara Barton Papers*, Library of Congress, Washington, D.C.

CHAPTER 2
Learning the Value of Selflessness

1. Elizabeth B. Pryor, *Clara Barton: Professional Angel* (Philadelphia: University of Pennsylvania Press, 1988), p. 6.
2. Ibid., p. 5.
3. Clara Barton, *The Story of My Childhood* (Meriden, Conn.: Journal Publishing, 1907), p. 32.
4. Quoted in "Clara Barton Copybook," ca. 1830, in *Clara Barton Papers*, Library of Congress, Washington, D.C.
5. Barton, *The Story of My Childhood*, p. 56.
6. Ibid., pp. 51–52.

7. Ibid., pp. 77–78.

CHAPTER 3
A Truly Gifted Teacher

1. Quoted in "The Clara Barton Home," in *Church Messenger*, May 7, 1896, clipping in *Clara Barton Papers*, Library of Congress, Washington, D.C.
2. Clara Barton, *The Story of My Childhood* (Meriden, Conn.: Journal Publishing, 1907), p. 119.
3. Quoted in a letter to Mrs. J. H. Balcom, January 20, 1911, in *Clara Barton Papers*, Library of Congress, Washington, D.C.
4. Quoted in an untitled article in the *New York Daily Tribune*, August 21, 1898, in *Clara Barton Papers*, Library of Congress, Washington, D.C.
5. *Centennial History of the Town of Millbury*, Massachusetts (Millbury, Mass.: Town Press, 1915), p. 333.
6. William E. Barton, *The Life of Clara Barton, Founder of the American Red Cross* (New York: AMS, 1969), vol. 1, pp. 83–84.
7. Elizabeth B. Pryor, *Clara Barton: Professional Angel* (Philadelphia: University of Pennsylvania Press, 1988), p. 47.
8. Ibid., p. 54.

CHAPTER 4
Coming to the Aid of Her Country

1. Quoted in an unpublished interview between Clara Barton and Leonora Halstead, July 29, 1890, in *Clara Barton Papers*, Library of Congress, Washington, D.C.
2. Ibid.
3. Stephen B. Oates, *A Woman of Valor: Clara Barton and the Civil War* (New York: Free Press, 1994), p. 10.
4. Oates, p. 11.

5. William E. Barton, *The Life of Clara Barton, Founder of the American Red Cross* (New York: AMS, 1969), vol. 1, p. 110.
6. Letter to Stephen Barton, March 1, 1862, quoted in Oates, p. 39.
7. Letter to Fannie Childs, April 25, 1861, in *Clara Barton Papers*, Library of Congress, Washington, D.C.
8. Oates, p. 22.
9. Ibid., pp. 61–62.
10. Ibid., p. 47.
11. Quoted in Halstead interview.

CHAPTER 5

Into the Heat of Battle

1. Letter to General Q.A. Gillmore, September 18, 1863, in National Archives and Records Service, Washington, D.C.
2. Stephen B. Oates, *A Woman of Valor: Clara Barton and the Civil War* (New York: Free Press, 1994), p. 63.
3. Letter to Henry Wilson, April 7, 1864, in *Clara Barton Papers*, Library of Congress, Washington, D.C.
4. Oates, p. 70.

CHAPTER 6

A Relentless Search for the Missing

1. Elizabeth B. Pryor, *Clara Barton: Professional Angel* (Philadelphia: University of Pennsylvania Press, 1988), p. 136.
2. Abraham Lincoln, *Collected Works*, ed. Roy P. Basler (Westport, Conn.: Greenwood Press, 1974), vol. 8, p. 423.
3. Clara Barton, "To the People," quoted in Stephen B. Oates, *A Woman of Valor: Clara Barton and the Civil War* (New York: Free Press, 1994), p. 311.
4. Oates, pp. 367–368.

5. Quoted in Clara Barton, *Diary,* in *Clara Barton Papers,* Library of Congress, Washington, D.C.

CHAPTER 7
Creation of the American Red Cross

1. Elizabeth B. Pryor, *Clara Barton: Professional Angel* (Philadelphia: University of Pennsylvania Press, 1988), p. 157.
2. Ibid., p. 159.
3. Clara Barton, *The Red Cross: A History* (Washington, D.C.: American Red Cross, 1898), p. 62.
4. Ibid., pp. 36, 41.
5. Ibid., p. 100.
6. Ibid., p. 67.
7. Ibid., pp. 13–14.
8. Pryor, p. 211.

CHAPTER 8
Barton's Red Cross in Action

1. Clara Barton, *The Red Cross: A History* (Washington, D.C.: American Red Cross, 1898), p. 108.
2. Ibid., p. 113.
3. Ibid., p. 134.
4. Ibid., p. 197.
5. Elizabeth B. Pryor, *Clara Barton: Professional Angel* (Philadelphia: University of Pennsylvania Press, 1988), p. 275.
6. Barton, p. 234.
7. Ibid., p. 101.
8. Ibid., p. 117.
9. Ibid., p. 524.
10. Pryor, p. 324.
11. Barton, p. 14.

CHAPTER 9
Final Battles and a Living Legacy

1. Elizabeth B. Pryor, *Clara Barton: Professional Angel* (Philadelphia: University of Pennsylvania Press, 1988), p. 350.

2. Elizabeth H. Turner, "Clara Barton and Formation of Public Policy in Galveston, 1900," n.d., <http://archive.rockefeller.edu/publications/conferences/turner.pdf> (August 9, 2007).

3. PBS interview of Jeffrey Brown by Elizabeth H. Turner, September 21, 2005, <http://www.pbs.org/newshour/bb/weather/july-dec05/galveston_9-21.html> (August 9, 2007).

4. William E. Barton, *The Life of Clara Barton, Founder of the American Red Cross* (New York: AMS, 1969), vol. 2, p. 374.

5. "Monument Text," *Clara Barton Monument at Antietam National Battlefield*, n.d., < http://www.nps.gov/archive/anti/monuments/Clara_B.htm> (November 30, 2007).

6. Clara Barton, *The Red Cross: A History* (Washington, D.C.: American Red Cross, 1898), p. 168.

GLOSSARY

amputation—The removal of a limb or other body part.

anxious—Worried or nervous.

bleeding—A medical practice where a doctor drained blood from a patient. The belief was that this would effect a cure by removing impure substances from the body.

boarding school—A school where the students live in dorms on the school grounds instead of in their homes.

carnage—Terrible bloodshed and death.

deplorable—Awful or disgraceful.

front—In a war, the place where the opposing forces meet and do battle.

hallmark—A sign, trait, or symbol typically displayed by a person or group.

humanitarian—Charitable, kindly, and/or generous and giving.

international—Having to do with many or all nations; global.

monstrosity—Something that is terrible.

neutrals—People, organizations, or countries that do not choose sides during a war.

AMERICANS: *The Spirit of a Nation*

pitiable—Sad or pathetic.

prophet—A person who bears a message from God or foretells future events.

quartermaster—In armies and in other military organizations, an officer or agency that issues various supplies to the troops.

ratify—To legally accept or approve something.

recuperate—To recover from an illness.

reimburse—To repay someone.

selectman—An elected town official.

selfless—Unselfish; concerned with others rather than oneself.

substandard—Of poor or unacceptable quality.

switch—A thin, flexible tree branch used to beat someone.

unorthodox—Very unusual.

FURTHER READING

Books

Collier, James Lincoln. *The Clara Barton You Never Knew.* New York: Children's Press, 2003.

Ditchfield, Christin. *Clara Barton: Founder of the American Red Cross.* New York: Franklin Watts, 2004.

Dolan, Edward. *The Spanish-American War.* Brookfield, Conn.: Millbrook Press, 2001.

Gallagher, Jim. *The Johnstown Flood.* New York: Chelsea House, 2000.

Hughes, Chris. *The Battle of Antietam.* San Diego: Blackbirch Press, 2001.

Marko, Eve. *Clara Barton and the American Red Cross.* Edina, Minn.: Abdo, 2005.

Turk, Michele. *Blood, Sweat and Tears: An Oral History of the Red Cross.* New York: E Street Press, 2006.

INTERNET ADDRESSES

American Red Cross History Museum
   <http://www.redcross.org/museum/history/>

Clara Barton Birthplace Museum—Kid's Corner
   **<http://208.67.82.76.clarabartonbirthplace.org/
   kids_corner>**

Clara Barton National Historic Site
   <http://www.nps.gov/archive/clba/house.htm>

INDEX